WHAT PRICE CLEAN AIR?

A Market Approach to Energy and Environmental Policy

A Statement by the Research and Policy Committee of the Committee for Economic Development

Committee for Economic Development. Research and Policy Committee. What Price Clean Air?
A Market Approach to Energy and Environmental Policy: a statement by the Research and
Policy Committee of the Committee for Economic Development.

First printing in bound-book form: 1993
Paperback: $15.00
Printed in the United States of America
Design: Rowe & Ballantine

COMMITTEE FOR ECONOMIC DEVELOPMENT
477 Madison Avenue, New York, NY 10022
(212) 688-2063

2000 L Street, N.W., Washington, DC 20006
(202) 296-5860

CONTENTS

WHAT PRICE CLEAN AIR?
A Market Approach to Energy and Environmental Policy

RESEARCH AND POLICY COMMITTEE

viii

PURPOSE OF THIS STATEMENT

What Price Clean Air? is being released at a time when both energy and environmental policies are being reconsidered and many policy makers are urging a fundamental reevaluation of the nation's approach to environmental quality. We applaud this new willingness to look for better ways to achieve a clean environment at an appropriate cost.

It is imperative that the nation receive the most value possible from the resources it devotes to environmental purposes. While market-based mechanisms rather than traditional command-and-control regulations present a way to improve environmental quality at the least cost, attempts at such reform have often been blocked by inertia and political opposition. It is now essential that policy makers recognize the importance of achieving environmental quality at lower cost.

What Price Clean Air? discusses air quality, energy use, and environmental policy in the United States. The aim of the statement is to propose a framework for environmental policy centered on more affordable and effective market incentives that promote clean air and energy conservation.

The subcommittee that produced this report (see page viii) represents an unusual collaboration of business, environmental, academic, and public policy organizations. Only CED trustees are responsible for the report's recommendations. Important differences remain between the views of the trustees and those of the environmental and academic experts advising CED. However, there were significant areas of agreement among all of the participants, particularly on the use of market solutions to deal with environmental and energy problems.

As the policy statement is being released, energy tax proposals are being considered for both their environmental and revenue effects. This report, however, focuses on the most cost-effective means of improving environ-mental conditions. It is not about reducing the federal budget deficit, and it does not address such measures as the proposed Btu tax, the primary objective of which is to raise revenues.

While such energy taxes can have environmental effects, the Btu tax is not the most cost-effective method of reducing pollution because it affects nonpolluting energy sources and discriminates among fossil fuels on the basis of heat content rather than on environmental effects. Instead, the report states that a tax on the carbon content of fuels would be the most effective means of achieving large reductions in greenhouse gases.

In evaluating energy tax proposals, including the modified Btu tax proposed by the Clinton Administration, policy makers concerned with energy and environmental policy may want to consider not only the revenue effects but also the environmental consequences of these taxes, with emphasis on the principles of environmental regulation put forth in this report.

A HISTORY OF CONCERN

Energy and environmental concerns are not new to CED. Over the past two decades, CED has issued several reports on these subjects, including *More Effective Programs for a Cleaner Environment* (1974), *Thinking Through the Energy Problem* (1979), by Thomas C. Schelling, Professor of Economics at the University of Maryland, and *Energy Prices and Public Policy* (1982), which CED prepared jointly with The Conservation Foundation. When the CED trustees expressed a renewed interest in energy and its environmental implications a few years ago, CED sponsored a 1989 conference on the theme "Promising Directions for Future U.S. Policies on Energy and the Environment" at the Department of Energy. As an outgrowth of this conference and strong general trustee interest, CED organized the subcommittee responsible for this policy statement.

ACKNOWLEDGEMENTS

I would like to express the deep appreciation of the Research and Policy Committee to Thomas A. Vanderslice, Chairman and Chief Executive Officer of M/A-Com Inc., for chairing the subcommittee that produced this report. His leadership on this project from the design phase to completion was outstanding. The Committee is also extremely grateful to the participating subcommittee members, non-trustee members, and advisors, all of whom lent an extraordinarily broad range of expertise and opinion to this project.

Very special thanks are due to Project Director William J. Beeman, CED Vice President and Director of Economic Studies; Project Associate Michael K. Baker, CED Policy Analyst; and Project Staff Member Carol Alvey, CED Administrative Assistant, for steering the report to completion.

Finally, we must thank the funders whose generous support made this project possible: Charles Stewart Mott Foundation, Philip D. Reed Endowment Fund at CED, ARCO Foundation, Consolidated Edison Company of New York, Inc., Entergy Corporation, Ford Motor Company Fund, General Electric Foundation, General Motors Foundation, Nissan North America, Inc., Phillips Petroleum Foundation, Inc., Potlatch Corporation, Shell Oil Company, and Texaco Foundation.

Josh S. Weston
Chairman
CED Research and Policy Committee

Chapter 1

INTRODUCTION AND SUMMARY OF POLICY

The quality of the environment has a profound effect on the well-being of both current and future citizens of every country. Therefore, protecting the environment should be a high priority for all nations. The challenge is to achieve and maintain a high quality environment without deterring economic progress. Because activities that create pollution, such as energy consumption, tend to rise with economic growth, the problem is particularly difficult for poor countries that are trying to improve their economies and living standards. This does not mean that economic progress and environmental protection are incompatible goals. Indeed, air quality and most other environmental conditions are generally better in advanced industrial countries than in developing countries because economic growth provides the resources for improving environmental conditions.

Substantial progress has been made in the United States during the last few decades in reducing air pollution, but the job of improving air quality is not complete. CED believes that this nation has an obligation to current and future generations to achieve cleaner air and to work with other nations to find solutions to the problem of global climate change. But we also need to develop consistent policies and cost-effective regulations based upon sound economic principles. The cost of environmental regulations is now rising very rapidly, and future measures to deal with global climate change could add substantially to these costs, to the point of seriously slowing the pace of economic growth even in developed nations. Consequently, there is an urgent need for regulatory reform to reduce excessive compliance costs and make environmental controls more effective. We believe that environmental quality can and should be improved without imposing an undue burden on the economy.

This policy statement focuses on one aspect of environmental policy: energy use and its effects on air quality. It describes current regulatory practices in the United States for maintaining air quality, with emphasis on opportunities to improve their effectiveness. Given the competition for scarce resources from other social needs, this statement urges adopting more cost-effective regulatory methods that will permit the resources available for environmental protection to be used most efficiently. **The basic economic principles underlying our specific recommendations are that benefit-cost analysis should be the basis for establishing environmental standards and that market-based mechanisms, such as emission taxes and tradable permits, are generally preferable to inefficient command-and-control methods of regulation.**

IMPROVED AIR, HIGHER COSTS

The national program to reduce urban air pollution has had a large impact on air quality in the United States. Emissions of most major pollutants have declined substantially in the last two decades, and consequently, ambient air concentrations of major pollutants have fallen sharply (see Figures 1 and 2). Moreover, the 1990 Clean Air Act Amendments represent a major additional commitment to cleaner air, which will produce further dramatic improvements by the end of the decade, according to Environmental Protection Agency (EPA) projections. But the costs are large and rising. The direct cost of complying with environmental regulations was about $115 billion in 1990, of which about $30 billion was spent on air quality (see Figure 3). The 1990 Amendments to the Clean Air Act are expected to add at least $20 billion a year to the cost of environmental protection by the end of the decade. This in-

POLICY RECOMMENDATIONS

The principles of regulation espoused in this report have led us to propose significant changes in the approach to U.S. environmental regulation. Reflecting our preference for market-based control mechanisms over command-and-control regulations, **CED recommends consideration of a motor vehicle emission charge program and implementation of a motor vehicle scrappage program. The former should be implemented if further action is needed beyond that required by the 1990 Clean Air Act to reduce pollution from motor vehicles. The scrappage program would be for old automobiles, which contribute disproportionately to air pollution.**

CED also supports policies to encourage cost-effective renewable energy technologies and improved efficiency in energy use as a means to reduce both local pollution and greenhouse gas (GHG) emissions.

Developing sound policies to deal with global climate change is difficult, in part, because of the scientific uncertainty concerning this issue. Clearly, high-cost control measures should be implemented only if the scientific evidence confirms that global climate change is a serious threat to society. **After careful consideration, CED has concluded that this uncertainty argues for flexible policies, not inaction. Indeed, we recommend that a comprehensive contingency plan for mitigating GHG emissions be developed promptly. Top priority should be given to increased research to reduce scientific uncertainty and to the implementation of a number of low-cost policies that will reduce GHG emissions.** This would include such actions as the elimination of existing subsidies on the production and consumption of fuels with high carbon content. If future experience and scientific research indicate that low-cost methods of reducing GHG emissions are insufficient and that much more stringent control measures are needed, **CED recommends that U.S. regulators turn to market-based incentives to control GHG emissions rather than to command-and-control mechanisms. The principles of regulation that we support indicate that a tax on the carbon content of fossil fuels appears to be the most cost-effective method to achieve large reductions in emissions of carbon dioxide (CO_2), the principal man-made GHG.**

However, more study is needed concerning problems of implementing a carbon tax. For example, without an international agreement to coordinate carbon taxes and other emission control mechanisms, a carbon tax would not be an effective control instrument, and its economic effects could put some nations that adopt it at a serious competitive disadvantage. **Consequently, we recommend that the economic effects of implementing a carbon tax and other possible market-based mechanisms, such as tradable emission permits, be studied further.* If any such mechanism is adopted, great care must be taken to minimize or offset any unintended adverse consequences and to ensure that the desired environmental goals are met.**

We also believe that nuclear and renewable energy sources offer environmental and other advantages which make them feasible and attractive alternatives to fossil fuels. For the most part, these energy sources generate no net emissions of GHGs and smog- or acid-forming pollutants. They could help to reduce U.S. dependence on foreign oil and keep the U.S. energy base diversified. For these reasons, **CED recommends that nuclear power be retained as an option, and we support efforts to make it more cost-effective. We also encourage increased research to make renewable energy more cost-effective.**

*See memorandum by FRANKLIN A. LINDSAY (page 93).

crease in costs is driven largely by two factors: (1) Compliance costs tend to rise more sharply as air quality standards are tightened and more stringent controls become necessary; and (2) with a few notable exceptions, U.S. policy makers continue to rely on inefficient command-and-control regulations for reducing pollution rather than on the more flexible and far less costly mechanisms recommended in this statement. If the nation decides to address the issue of climate change aggressively by controlling greenhouse gas (GHG) emissions, the cost of controlling air quality will be substantially higher.

Figure 1

Change in U.S. Emissions
Major Pollutants, Selected Periods

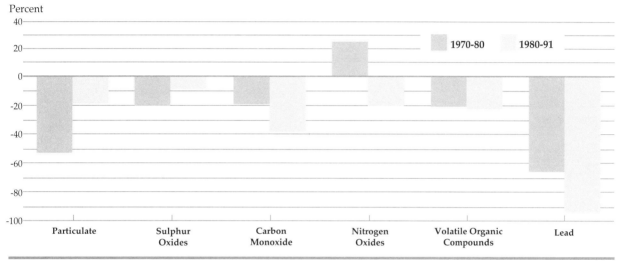

SOURCE: Environmental Protection Agency

Figure 2

Change in U.S. Ambient Air Concentrations
Major Pollutants, Selected Periods

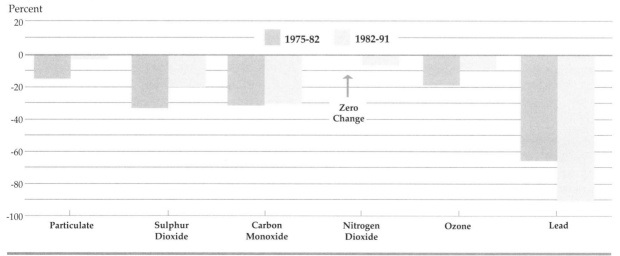

SOURCE: Environmental Protection Agency

3

Figure 3

Direct Costs of Pollution Control in the United States

Estimates for 1972-2000, in constant dollars

Billions of 1990 dollars

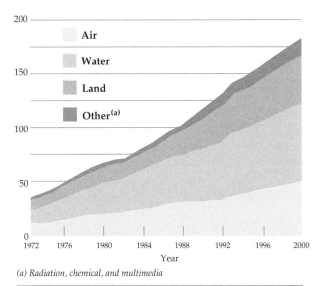

(a) Radiation, chemical, and multimedia

SOURCE: Environmental Protection Agency

MAKING REGULATION MORE COST-EFFECTIVE

Given the outlook for rising regulatory costs, it makes sense to use the most cost-effective methods whenever regulation is necessary to protect the environment. Unfortunately, this is not the practice of the current U.S. program for controlling air pollution. Standards for air quality and for emissions are often chosen without regard to their benefits and costs. In fact, the courts have ruled that the Clean Air Act *prohibits* regulators from weighing the benefits and costs to society when choosing national ambient air quality standards. **CED believes that such restrictions on benefit-cost analysis should be rescinded. We believe that targets for air quality should be chosen after careful weighing of all benefits and costs in order to ensure that our resources are not wasted on measures that provide no net benefit to society.**

Regulators have generally also failed to employ the least-cost **control mechanisms.**

They have not given equal treatment to emissions from different pollution sources, and their emphasis has been on technical control mechanisms, rather than market-based incentives to discourage emissions. Even the 1990 Clean Air Act Amendments (which do provide a market-based control mechanism to reduce emissions that cause acid rain) continue to place primary emphasis on command-and-control regulations. For example, the new regulations on urban ozone, a persistent problem in some areas, place more emphasis on mobile sources of pollution than on stationary sources, and they emphasize emissions technology instead of market-based controls. As a consequence, compliance costs are expected to greatly exceed the benefits of the program. **CED believes that a considerable saving could be achieved by examining the Clean Air Act to determine which specific objectives can be accomplished in a way consistent with the criteria for efficient pollution control recommended in this statement.**

Studies have shown that enormous reductions in the nation's compliance costs could be achieved by adopting regulations that apply equally to emissions from all sources and by using more flexible market incentives, such as **emission charges** and **tradable emission permits**, to control pollution.[1] Emission charges and tradable permits take advantage of the large differentials in abatement costs among polluters and encourage those polluters with low compliance costs to make larger cutbacks in emissions. Such control mechanisms automatically minimize *total* compliance costs.[2] **Because it is virtually *impossible* for regulators to achieve this least-cost outcome with command-and-control regulations, CED strongly recommends market-based mechanisms for controlling emissions.**

Unlike many command-and-control regulations, market-based regulations not only discourage activities that cause emissions but also strongly encourage experimentation to develop lower-cost technologies to reduce pollution. In addition, market-based incentives encourage consumers and producers to become more energy-efficient, often the most cost-effective method of reducing pollution. Market-based controls also encourage producers and consumers to substitute low-polluting fuels for "dirty" fuels and renewable energy sources for fossil fuels.

CED believes that every effort should be made to make visible all costs and benefits of regulation so that society can make wise choices. Of course, the costs of emission charges and tradable permits are generally far more visible than those of command-and-control regulations. **Moreover, public resources available for environmental protection should be concentrated on those activities that cannot be adequately funded by the private sector, such as research and development, and on regulations that offer the greatest "bang for the buck."**

MOTOR VEHICLE EMISSIONS AND FUEL EFFICIENCY

Regulations controlling motor vehicle emissions are among the most important and costly programs undertaken to improve local air quality. These programs have achieved sharp reductions in motor vehicle emissions, but they have not been cost-effective because their design violates fundamental regulatory principles. Emission control mechanisms are applied to motor vehicle technology and performance rather than to actual emissions. Consequently, compliance costs are not closely related to the quantity of emissions. Once the technology is in place, there is often no incentive to take further steps to reduce emissions. Thus, having purchased a car with a catalytic converter, the owner may experience little difference in emission control costs whether the vehicle is driven 1,000 miles or 100,000 miles a year. By contrast, market-based incentives, such as emission charges and energy taxes, directly discourage driving, which causes emissions. Emission charges also encourage the purchase of equipment with the most cost-effective emissions technology.

The 1990 Amendments to the Clean Air Act mandate changes in automobile technology and reformulated fuels in certain urban areas in order to bring them into compliance with air quality standards. Reformulated gasoline will not only reduce emissions directly but will also discourage driving because reformulation will substantially raise the price of gasoline. If further emission reductions are justified, CED urges regulators to turn to cost-effective market-based control mechanisms. **One measure deserving serious consideration is an emission charge program for areas that do not meet federal standards for air quality. Although emission charges could efficiently lower pollution, the potentially high administrative costs of such a program and its impact on low-income drivers need to be clarified.**

The Clean Air Act already mandates emissions inspections in about 180 cities in 37 states, and therefore, an emission charge program need not involve unacceptable additional administrative costs. An advantage of an emission charge program is that it would force improvements in existing inspection procedures for motor vehicles. The failure of current programs to require proper maintenance of emission control equipment means that the benefits of improved control mechanisms are often not being realized. **CED also recommends that state and local governments consider substituting emission charges for existing personal property taxes and other fees on automobiles.** Unlike these taxes, an emission charge would discourage the use of older "dirty" vehicles that emit large amounts of pollution.

CED also favors the development of a scrappage program, whereby owners of high-polluting vehicles in nonattainment areas[3] would be offered a bounty for the vehicles. A scrappage program could deliver large savings if firms receive marketable emission credits (for purchasing these vehicles) that can be used to comply with other emission requirements.

One problem with an emission charge is that it would be higher for high-polluting older vehicles, which are frequently owned by lower-income individuals. However, the regressive tendency of an emission charge could be alleviated by the addition of a scrappage program if a high enough price is paid for the high-polluting vehicles.

The effectiveness of federal regulations on motor vehicle fuel efficiency has also been limited by confusion over the ultimate goal of these regulations and by reliance on inefficient controls. Originally, corporate average fuel economy (CAFE) standards were proposed as a means of limiting the demand for gasoline at a time when gasoline prices were held artificially low by price controls. With the expiration of price controls and, more recently, with diminishing concern about oil imports, advocates of CAFE shifted their concern to urban smog and global climate change. However, CAFE is not a cost-effective regulatory instrument for dealing with either of these environmental issues. A recent study by the National Research Council pointed out that smog-causing emissions are not directly affected by CAFE because CAFE is intended to minimize the consumption of fuel rather than emissions per mile driven. Since emissions standards are stated in grams per mile, they are identical for every vehicle regardless of fuel economy.[4] CAFE also is not a cost-effective instrument for dealing with global climate change, since it affects only gasoline consumption in new vehicles, which account for only a small fraction of GHG emissions. Furthermore, CAFE does not discourage driving and may, in fact, raise total vehicle miles travelled by lowering the cost per mile driven.

CAFE has proved to be an extremely expensive regulatory program with enormous hidden costs and very limited effectiveness as an environmental measure. **CED opposes proposals to increase CAFE standards because it believes that other mechanisms described in this report can achieve the same environmental objectives more effectively and at much lower cost.**

GLOBAL CLIMATE CHANGE

The potential impact of greenhouse gas emissions on the earth's climate has recently emerged as a major international issue. The view of scientists assembled by the National Academy of Sciences and by the Intergovernmental Panel on Climate Change (IPCC) is that increased concentrations of these gases in the atmosphere could produce a significant change in the earth's climate, including a rise in average global temperatures, perhaps by the middle of the next century. But scientists are sharply divided about the magnitude of these effects. Some believe that the IPCC view of climate change is too pessimistic. There is even greater uncertainty about timing and regional distribution of potential effects on the climate. Currently, climate change projections are derived primarily from general circulation models, the reliability of which cannot easily be established. Although ongoing work continues to improve these models, they do not yet provide policy makers with a solid basis for gauging risks and for designing a clear-cut regulatory response.

The design and implementation of an appropriate regulatory response to climate change is complicated not only by scientific uncertainty but also by uncertainty concerning the economic and social consequences of climate change, the planet-wide nature of the problem, and the fact that man-made GHG emissions are generated by a wide range of basic economic activities that can be substantially curtailed only at great cost.

Some have proposed that any policy response to global climate change be postponed until the scientific issues are largely resolved. **However, we believe that uncertainty argues for the development of a comprehensive contingency plan for mitigating GHG emissions.** The objective of this plan should be to provide insurance against an environmental catastrophe, which appears to have a low probability but which the National Academy believes cannot be ruled out. **The highest priority should be given to scientific research in order to improve our understanding of global climate change and its effect on our economic and social institutions. The United States and the international community should also begin immediately to implement a number of low-cost mitigation measures,** including: (1) government policies to encourage cost-effective improvements in energy efficiency and the use of cost-effective renewable energy, (2) the elimination of government subsidies on high-carbon-content fuels, (3) the liberalization of trade in order to increase the availability of technology to improve pollution control, energy efficiency, and nonpolluting energy sources, (4) an international agreement to reduce deforestation, and (5) a program to reduce the growth in population worldwide.[5] If such low-cost measures are undertaken in many nations, we believe that the growth of CO_2 emissions will be reduced substantially.

Perhaps the greatest opportunity for low-cost reduction in CO_2 emissions exists in former Communist countries, where the end of subsidies and trade liberalization would encourage more efficient and less polluting energy use. The World Bank estimates that the removal of all energy subsidies throughout the world would cut CO_2 emissions by about 10 percent.

Most of the above low-cost measures should be undertaken for other reasons, regardless of the outlook for global climate change. **Regulators should turn to more stringent GHG abatement options only if these low-cost measures are found to be insufficient and future scientific research confirms that GHG emissions are a threat to society.** In principle, market-based incentives, such as emission charges or tradable emission permits, are the lowest-cost mechanisms for abating greenhouse emissions. If such measures are necessary, they should apply to all GHG emissions. But it is not easy to identify and control all GHG emissions, and in practice, a less inclusive mechanism may be necessary. **Indeed, among control options a tax on the carbon content of all fuels appears to be the most cost-effective abatement mechanism capable of achieving substantial reductions in GHG emissions.** Atmospheric concentrations of carbon dioxide account for about 55 percent of the greenhouse warming potential produced by human activity, and this share is expected to increase sharply. A carbon tax on all fuels, applied for convenience at the point of production or import, is about as close as one can get to a CO_2 emission tax.

However, there are many unresolved issues about the implementation of a carbon tax that require further study.* One of the more daunting aspects is that cooperation of countries with very diverse national interests is required. Action taken by a single nation or even a group of nations could easily be offset by others if there is no international agreement. An international agreement will be difficult to achieve, however, because the costs of reducing emissions are borne by individual countries while the benefits will accrue to the entire planet and probably will not be distributed regionally in the same way as costs. Moreover, it is not likely that all nations would employ the same control mechanisms; many would substitute other measures for a carbon tax, such as reductions in deforestation (a major source of CO_2)[6] or perhaps changes in agricultural practices that reduce emissions of methane. Poor nations might not cooperate unless advanced industrial nations agree to provide technical assistance and help them finance their abatement programs and the resultant economic losses. **Finally, consideration should be given to programs to encourage reduced population growth because increases in CO_2 emissions generated by continued rapid population growth would substantially offset the effects of CO_2 reductions from a carbon tax**.

The economic consequences of a carbon tax are also a critical issue. International agreements would be necessary to ensure that nations that adopt a carbon tax are not put at a competitive disadvantage in international markets compared to countries that employ other methods to reduce GHG emissions.** There is also the question of how to dispose of revenues from a carbon tax, which could be quite substantial. Some have proposed a revenue-neutral policy whereby revenue gains from a carbon tax would be offset by cuts in other existing taxes. The objective would be to improve the economic efficiency of the tax system and to minimize the macroeconomic effects. Finally, an adjustment assistance program may be necessary for those regions of the United States that are highly dependent on the

---

*See memorandum by LEON C. HOLT, JR. (page 93).

**See memorandum by FRANKLIN A. LINDSAY (page 93).

production of high-carbon-content fuels. **Thus, we recommend that the economic effects of implementing a carbon tax and other possible market-based mechanisms, such as tradable emission permits, be studied further. If any such mechanism is adopted, other policies may be needed to minimize or offset any unintended consequences of the chosen policy.**

In conclusion, CED believes that before **costly new regulatory programs, including fees, are implemented, additional scientific research is necessary to establish more clearly the dimensions of the threat of global climate change. Nevertheless, if low-cost methods of reducing greenhouse gases are found to be insufficient to deal with a serious threat to the global community, other more stringent options will have to be implemented as a means of achieving additional reductions.** A carbon fee, which appears to be the most cost-effective option for achieving additional reductions in CO_2, need not be large initially. An advantage of a market-based fee over command-and-control regulation is that it can be adjusted more flexibly as new information about climate change becomes available.

GASOLINE TAXES AND THE ENVIRONMENT

CED has endorsed the principle of imposing additional taxes on the consumption of products that demonstrably impose external health, safety, and environmental costs which exceed current levels of taxation.[7] Increased taxes that reflect "external costs," which are not included in the prices paid by consumers and producers but are borne instead by other members of society, may actually improve the efficiency of resource allocation. However, **CED has not endorsed increased gasoline taxes based on this principle because existing taxes and mandated cost increases enforced by the Clean Air Act of 1990 appear to reflect the social costs of pollution in many areas.**

Our analysis of air pollution indicates that increased gasoline taxes would be preferable to command-and-control regulations, such as increased CAFE, and that gasoline taxes would contribute to improved air quality because gasoline consumption would be discouraged. **However, CED does not recommend a gasoline tax purely as an environmental measure because increased gasoline taxes would not be the most cost-effective instrument for dealing with either local pollution or global climate change.*** Motor vehicle emissions have declined sharply in the last few decades, and when the 1990 Clean Air Act Amendments are implemented, motor vehicles may no longer be a major source of urban pollution.[8] Motor vehicle emissions are also a relatively small factor in the creation of GHG emissions. As indicated elsewhere in this report, global warming can be addressed much more effectively with a carbon tax. (Of course, a carbon tax would boost the price of gasoline as well as other fossil fuels.) An emission charge may also be more effective than gasoline taxes in dealing with local pollution.

Gasoline taxes would also generate substantial revenues for government and are sometimes recommended because of their combined environmental and fiscal effects. Proponents of increased gasoline taxes have argued that this tax is administratively simple and would help remedy air pollution, the trade imbalance, and the federal budget deficit all at once. For these reasons, some CED trustees favor gasoline taxes as a fiscal measure or as a combined economic and environmental measure. **However, this report does not take a position on a gasoline tax as a fiscal measure or as a means of reducing the trade deficit,** except to point out that the merits of such a tax can be judged only by comparison with the costs and benefits (including environmental) of other potential revenue sources — an issue that is beyond the scope of this statement.

ENERGY DEPENDENCE AND ENVIRONMENTAL GOALS

This country's heavy reliance on fossil fuels complicates both environmental and economic policies. Many are concerned that large oil imports make it difficult to promptly eliminate

---

*See memorandum by HAROLD A. POLING, MARTIN B. ZIMMERMAN, and GEORGE C. EADS (page 94).

the U.S. trade deficit, though oil imports are clearly only one component of the trade deficit and reductions in oil imports are not a necessary condition for achieving a trade balance in the long run (see "Oil Imports and the U.S. Trade Deficit" and Figure 4). The recent Gulf War and rising U.S. imports of oil have also renewed interest in U.S. economic security. No one can be sure how high prices would have gone had Saudi supplies been interrupted during the Gulf War.

Although petroleum imports declined after the 1979 price shock, they have risen rapidly since the mid-1980s. Net petroleum imports (net of exports), which rose to about 40 percent

of domestic consumption in 1991, are projected to rise more rapidly over the next few years (see Figure 5).[9] However, the rise in oil imports does not necessarily make the United States more vulnerable to oil price fluctuations. The market for oil is global, and changes in the world price would affect the domestic price even if the United States were completely self-sufficient in oil. Moreover, the risk of disruption in supplies appears to be reduced, at least for now, by the fact that energy supplies are now more abundant and the Middle East share of world oil production has declined. However, the Middle East possesses about two-thirds of the world's proven reserves, and some predict that the region's share of total production will rise (see Figure 6).

Given this situation, several nations have increased oil stockpiles as an insurance against disruption. Congress recently authorized an increase in the size of the U.S. Strategic Petroleum Reserve to provide a more substantial buffer for the U.S. economy against limited oil disruptions. This policy could be supplemented by actions to encourage the development of new oil reserves and other energy sources here and abroad.

OIL IMPORTS AND THE U.S. TRADE DEFICIT

Like other imported goods, oil imports contribute to the U.S. trade deficit. Although their share of total imports has declined (Figure 4), oil imports have reached record levels and now account for nearly one-third of the U.S. trade deficit. From 1986 to 1990, the cumulative U.S. trade deficit would have been $208 billion less without net petroleum imports. The rising U.S. debt to foreigners caused by our trade deficit is a serious concern, and the magnitude of oil imports does make it more difficult to correct the trade deficit. However, the recent experience of other nations demonstrates clearly that heavy dependence on a foreign commodity does not preclude a nation from running a trade surplus. Indeed, the problem of U.S. trade deficits in recent years has been primarily a consequence of macroeconomic policies and low national saving in the United States. CED has continually stated that a reduction in the federal budget deficit is the most important step that can be taken by the government to improve the competitiveness of U.S. industry in international markets. Reduced U.S. imports of oil could make a contribution to the trade and foreign debt problem of the United States, but macroeconomic action is a necessary condition for improving the competitiveness of U.S. industry and bringing the international current account into balance.

Figure 4

U.S. Petroleum Imports as a Percent of Total Imports, Selected Periods

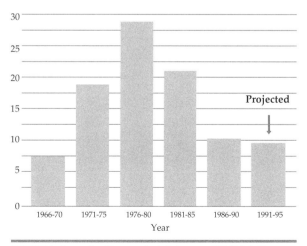

SOURCE: Council of Economic Advisers and DRI/McGraw-Hill

9

There is a coincidence of interests in reducing oil consumption by those concerned about U.S. dependence on foreign oil and those concerned about energy conservation and air quality. Many believe that the United States needs a more integrated approach to energy efficiency,

Figure 5

Net Petroleum Imports as a Percent of U.S. Petroleum Consumption, 1965-95

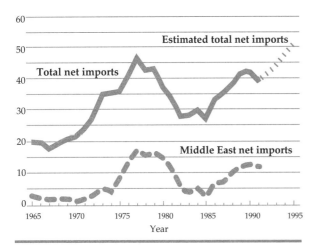

SOURCE: Energy Information Administration

Figure 6

Regional Oil Production as a Percent of World Total, Selected Years

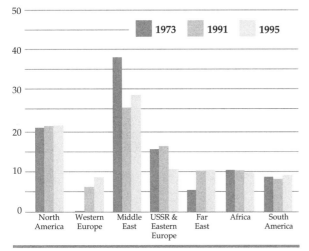

SOURCE: *BP Statistical Review of World Energy*, Congressional Research Service, and Energy Information Administration

environmental, and economic security policies in order to ensure that economic progress and clean air are both achieved. CED agrees that cost-effective energy efficiency improvements and the development of price-competitive nonpolluting energy sources should be high priorities for U.S. environmental policy (see Chapter 4). But the Strategic Petroleum Reserve appears to be the lowest-cost option for dealing with U.S. dependence on foreign oil. Although the economic security aspect of oil imports seems to be of diminished importance at the moment, political developments in the Middle East could reignite concern about oil disruptions.

SUMMARY OF RECOMMENDATIONS

This CED policy statement examines the current state of air quality and U.S. regulations pertaining to the atmosphere and energy use. It proposes reforms in selected areas of regulation that are needed to achieve high standards of air quality in the most cost-effective manner.

Chapter 2 is a description of the basic facts pertaining to energy use and air quality. Recent trends in the production and consumption of energy and in energy efficiency, developments in local air pollution, and the current state of knowledge about global climate change are covered briefly.

Chapter 3 compares the current regulatory philosophy pertaining to air quality control in the United States with principles of regulation that would permit regulators to achieve air quality goals in a cost-effective manner.

Chapter 4 applies the principles of regulation developed in the previous chapter to five current issues: (1) global climate change, (2) energy efficiency, (3) automobile fuel efficiency and emissions, (4) nuclear power, and (5) renewable energy sources.

The basic recommendations of the report can be summarized as follows:

PRINCIPLES OF REGULATION

1. The present approach to developing national standards for air quality and emissions, with its emphasis on techno-

logical prescriptions and elimination of all risk, is not a sound basis for choosing air quality goals. To the greatest degree possible, benefit-cost analysis should be employed to evaluate air quality and emission standards.

2. A given reduction in total emissions can be achieved at least cost if the incremental cost of reducing emissions is equalized across all sources. While it is virtually impossible for command-and-control mechanisms to achieve this least-cost outcome, two market mechanisms—emission charges and tradable emission permits—tend to automatically achieve this result when they are applied to all emission sources. When it is feasible, regulators should use these market mechanisms rather than command-and-control regulations to control air quality. Emission charges and tradable emission permits are also generally more effective for reducing pollution than a tax on fuels or subsidies, such as a special tax credit for pollution abatement equipment. This is because charges and permits aim directly at the quantity of emissions rather than indirectly at products whose by-products include emissions in varying degrees.

3. As far as is possible, control mechanisms should apply equally to all material sources of a given pollutant. Thus, for example, all emissions that significantly contribute to urban ozone should be treated equally, including those from stationary as well as mobile sources.

4. Sometimes the most cost-effective regulations can harm certain industries and regional employment. This problem should be addressed through economic adjustment policies rather than by employing inefficient regulation.

5. Many of the costs of regulation, such as the cost of automobile fuel economy regulations, are not readily apparent to the public. CED believes that regulators should make every effort to see that compliance costs are known so that wise decisions can be made.

6. Regulators should encourage the adoption of cost-effective energy-efficient measures as an alternative to the more costly "end-of-pipe" control equipment to reduce pollution.

GLOBAL CLIMATE CHANGE

1. CED believes that scientific uncertainty concerning the greenhouse effect does not justify a conclusion that all action should be postponed until the scientific issues are resolved. Indeed, a rational response to uncertainty in this very important intergenerational area is to insure against possible harm to succeeding generations with low-cost policies[10] that will reduce GHG emissions while also accomplishing other policy objectives.

2. CED believes that the U.S. government should develop a comprehensive contingency plan to reduce GHG emissions.* Top priority should be given to scientific research to reduce uncertainty and to implementing low-cost options for reducing GHG emissions, such as:

   - Improving energy efficiency in a cost-effective manner

   - Eliminating subsidies on the production or consumption of high-carbon-content fuels

   - Liberalizing trade in order to increase the availability of energy-efficient and pollution control technology, especially in developing countries and in former Communist countries

   - An international agreement to reduce deforestation

   - A program to reduce the growth in population worldwide

   CED also recommends accelerated research on the problems of implementing more complete control measures, particularly a carbon tax, which appears

---

*See memorandum by RICHARD J. KRUIZENGA (page 94).

to be the most effective instrument for achieving large reductions in GHG emissions.

3. The contingency plan should also include market-based control measures such as a carbon tax for achieving additional reductions in emissions. However, the United States should not put a carbon tax in place for environmental reasons unless future scientific research indicates that climate change is a serious threat to society and low-cost options prove to be inadequate. Moreover, the United States should not adopt such measures without the active participation of other advanced nations and without a program under way to encourage participation by developing countries.

ENERGY EFFICIENCY AND AIR QUALITY

1. Cost-effective energy efficiency investments are not only good business, they also are beneficial to the environment. However, the full potential for energy efficiency investments is not being realized for many different reasons. Government has a role to play in encouraging energy efficiency by (1) disseminating technical information, (2) supporting energy efficiency research, and (3) giving proper weight to the long-run benefits of cost-effective energy-efficient investments when making its own capital expenditures.

2. The federal government can promote "energy-efficient mortgages" in which additional loan financing is provided to buyers of homes with superior energy efficiency characteristics.

3. Government can also step up its efforts in such programs as energy efficiency labeling, by helping states develop up-to-date building codes, incentives for cost-effective electric utility conservation programs, and in a few instances, promulgating efficiency standards.

MOTOR VEHICLE FUEL EFFICIENCY AND EMISSIONS

1. Inefficient command-and-control regulations have been the primary controls for both vehicle fuel efficiency and emissions. Currently, some are proposing further mandatory increases in fuel efficiency (CAFE) as a means of reducing GHG emissions. CED finds that CAFE is a very inefficient method of dealing with air quality problems. Thus, we strongly oppose mandatory increases in CAFE.

2. Present emission control policy emphasizes engineering devices on motor vehicles, a costly and inefficient technology-based method of control. The 1990 Amendments to the Clean Air Act mandate further changes in motor vehicle technology and fuels. If future experience demonstrates that further controls are necessary, CED believes that states should consider the development of a cost-effective motor vehicle emission charge program for nonattainment areas. While administrative costs could be high, the potential efficiency gains justify serious consideration of such proposals. Because older vehicles account for a disproportionately high share of motor vehicle emissions, emission charges should replace those personal property taxes and other controls that encourage the aging of the vehicle fleet.

3. The Clean Air Act mandates more costly reformulated gasoline starting in 1995 for the nine urban areas with the most serious ozone problems. CED opposes the extension of these regulations beyond the nine cities already affected unless these requirements can be shown to be cost-effective. CED believes that potentially less costly methods of reducing urban smog, such as emission charges and the scrappage proposal described below, should be considered as alternatives.

4. The relatively high emission rates of older vehicles have led to a number of propos-

als for retiring these vehicles. CED recommends that a scrappage program, whereby a bounty would be offered to owners of old vehicles, be adopted in regions that have high levels of ground-level ozone. The program could be paid for by permitting businesses to purchase the old vehicles in return for marketable emission credits. This would allow firms to substitute emission reductions from vehicle scrappage for more costly emission reductions from other sources.

5. While increased gasoline taxes are preferable to command-and-control regulations such as increased CAFE, CED does not recommend higher gasoline taxes as a purely environmental control measure because they would not be the most cost-effective instrument for dealing with either local pollution or global climate change.

NUCLEAR ENERGY

1. New nuclear power plants can and should be made more cost-effective, and excessive public concerns about safety should be addressed. Although regulatory oversight is important, vigorous self-policing and standardization by the nuclear industry are also critical. Poor performers should be strongly encouraged by the industry watchdog organization, the Institute of Nuclear Power Operations (INPO), to live up to the high standards that the industry sets for itself.

2. The United States should provide substantial technical assistance to upgrade unsafe nuclear reactors in other countries, and world bodies should participate in technical and financial support. Many

reactors in Eastern Europe and the former Soviet Union pose a threat to the health and safety of their own and neighboring populations. Although the technology and operational standards of these reactors are often inferior to those used in the United States, another accident such as that at Chernobyl may serve a devastating blow to the U.S. nuclear industry.

3. Precertified standardized plant designs and combined construction permits and operating licenses are crucial to reduce construction times and capital costs and to give nuclear plant buyers greater assurance of making a return on their investment. Standardized designs also foster cheaper subsequent improvements in safety and retrofitting.

4. The federal government should fulfill its mandate to identify a sound, safe, permanent repository for nuclear waste. Regulators should encourage residents near proposed sites to accept safe repositories by offering them adequate financial inducements.

RENEWABLE ENERGY

1. Renewable energy sources promise to contribute to the future U.S. energy base. Indeed, some renewable energy sources are already cost-effective. But others are not yet cost-effective or are only marginally so. Many of the obstacles to cost-effective renewable energy may be overcome by an effective research and development program. The federal government has a crucial role to play in this effort by providing tax incentives for R&D in general and through direct funding of renewable energy R&D.

Chapter 2

ENERGY USE AND THE ATMOSPHERE: THE BASIC FACTS

During the last 30 years, the public and private sectors in the United States have devoted enormous resources to environmental protection. The total annual cost reached about $115 billion in 1990, of which nearly 30 percent was dedicated to improving air quality. The outcome of this effort has been mixed. Thanks to emission controls and more efficient energy use, emissions and national ambient air concentrations of pollutants have been substantially reduced. But the improvement has not been universal; air quality remains unsatisfactory in many areas. Nevertheless, the prospects for further progress in air quality are quite good. The 1990 Amendments to the Clean Air Act will result in reduced air pollution in the United States. The Montreal Protocol will produce a decline in chlorofluorocarbon (CFC) emissions, which appear to be responsible for stratospheric ozone depletion. However, the nation now faces a more complex environmental issue: the development of appropriate policies relating to the emission of greenhouse gases (GHGs). The 1992 United Nations Conference on Environment and Development (UNCED) in Brazil demonstrated widespread support for some steps to decrease pollution and reduce man-made emissions of GHGs.

This chapter describes trends in energy use and air quality. We begin with energy use, as it is well known that energy consumption accounts for a large part of the air pollution problem and is a major source of GHG emissions. The objective of presenting these basic facts is to provide a foundation for the discussion in later chapters concerning policy goals and prescriptions.

TRENDS IN INTERNATIONAL ENERGY CONSUMPTION

World consumption of energy has doubled since 1965, and the U.S. Department of Energy projects a further increase of about one-third by the year 2010.[1] The regional distribution of consumption has been changing, with a diminution of demand growth in the member countries of the Organization for Economic Cooperation and Development (OECD) and an acceleration of growth in many developing countries.[2] Consequently, the OECD's share of total energy consumption has declined from 62 percent in 1970 to 52 percent in 1991 (see Figure 7). This trend is expected to continue as developed countries become increasingly efficient energy users and as developing nations become more populous, urbanized, and industrialized.

The countries that still have, or until recently did have, centrally planned economies accounted for about 30 percent of world energy consumption in 1991.[3] Future demand in these countries is particularly difficult to project because the success of their economic renewal programs is uncertain. However, they generally have been very inefficient energy users, largely because of subsidies that make energy available at well below market prices. Thus, there are great opportunities for improvement as these states move toward market economies. If these opportunities are realized, they are expected to offset growth in demand for energy resulting from increasing prosperity.

Oil currently accounts for about 39 percent of the world's primary energy consumption.

Figure 7

Regional Energy Consumption as a Percent of World Total, Selected Years

Percent

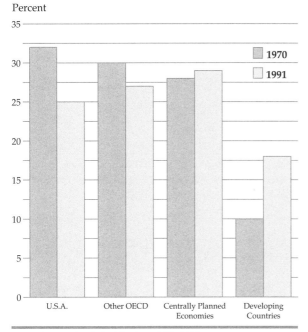

SOURCE: *BP Statistical Review of World Energy*

Although growth of demand for oil is likely to remain strong over the next 20 years, it is expected to decline slightly in importance relative to natural gas (currently 21 percent), nuclear energy (6 percent), and other nonfossil fuels (7 percent). Coal's share is forecast to remain approximately the same at about 26 percent.[4]

TRENDS IN DOMESTIC CONSUMPTION

The United States now consumes 25 percent of the world's energy, down from 34 percent in 1960 and 32 percent in 1970. This decline reflects demographic and economic trends as well as substantial improvements in energy efficiency. U.S. energy consumption since World War II has gone through two distinct phases. The first, up to 1973, was characterized by steady growth from 30 quadrillion British thermal units (Btus) to 74 quadrillion Btus, driven by sharply rising demand for petroleum and natural gas throughout the period (see Figure 8). The second, from 1973 to the present,

Figure 8

U.S. Energy Consumption by Fuel, 1950-91

Quadrillion btu

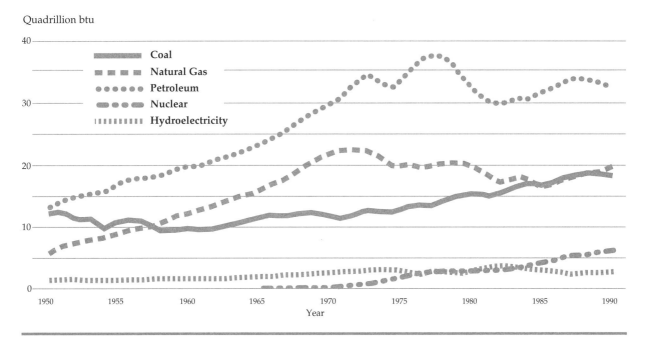

SOURCE: Energy Information Administration

15

was characterized by lower growth of aggregate consumption and a concomitant decline in the relative shares of petroleum and natural gas from 77 percent to 65 percent. As Table 1 shows, the widespread substitution of coal and nuclear energy for petroleum and natural gas in the production of electricity was of major importance in the declining shares of the latter two fuels. Electrification of the U.S. economy continued steadily throughout the entire post-war period. Electricity provided 15 percent of delivered energy in 1991 and accounted for 37 percent of all primary energy consumed.

Figure 9 shows the growth of aggregate energy consumption since 1950 on a sectoral basis. The flattening of the curves after 1973 in all three sectors hints at substantial progress in energy efficiency.

ENERGY EFFICIENCY IN THE UNITED STATES

On a per capita basis, U.S. energy consumption has declined 8 percent from its peak just before the second round of major oil price hikes in 1979. Nevertheless, partly because of lower energy prices, U.S. per capita consumption remains considerably above the OECD average and is exceeded only by Canada's among the developed countries (see Figure 10). A commonly used measure of energy efficiency is the ratio of energy consumption to gross domestic product (GDP). For the United States, this ratio has improved 27 percent since 1973 (after a long period in which it was roughly constant).[5] The U.S. efficiency gains have been part of an OECD-wide trend (see Figure 11).

However, country-to-country comparisons of measures such as energy consumption per capita and energy/GDP ratios should be interpreted with care because they fail to take into account factors such as differing population densities and distribution of output among economic sectors. For example, the United States transportation sector uses more energy per capita than any of the other Group of Seven (G-7) countries, but that is partly because U.S. population density is the second lowest. Japan, on the other hand, has the lowest transportation consumption per capita and the highest population density.[6]

Energy efficiency in the United States registered gains in the years immediately after both oil price shocks, although efficiency improvements in manufacturing predate the oil price turbulence of the 1970s and appear to reflect longer-term competitive pressures more than sensitivity to temporary energy market upheavals.[7]

Table 1

Electric Utility Generation, by Fuel, as a Percent of Total Generation, Selected Years

	1950	1973	1991
Coal	47	46	55
Natural Gas	14	18	9
Petroleum	10	17	4
Nuclear Power	0	4	22
Renewables	29	15	10

SOURCE: Energy Information Administration

Figure 9

U.S. Energy Consumption by Sector, 1950-91

Quadrillion btu

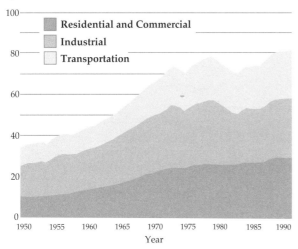

SOURCE: Energy Information Administration

Figure 10

Energy Consumption Per Capita
Selected OECD Countries, 1970-91

Tons of oil equivalent

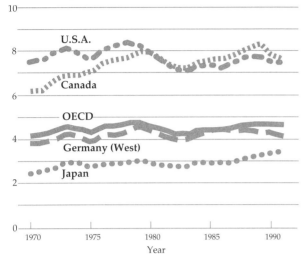

Tons are metric tons; 1 metric ton of oil equivalent = 10 million kilocalories (kcal).

SOURCE: International Energy Agency

Figure 11

Energy Intensity, Selected OECD Countries
Ratio of Energy Consumption to Real GDP, 1970-91

toe/thousands of 1985 dollars

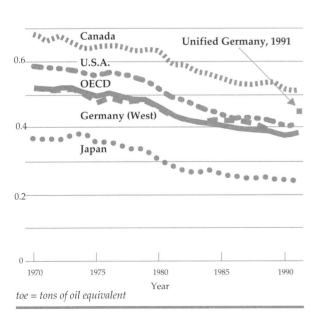

toe = tons of oil equivalent

SOURCE: International Energy Agency

The improvement in energy efficiency in the United States since 1973 is attributable to several factors. Technological advances, such as more efficient motor vehicles, industrial processes, and home appliances, and wider application of preexisting technologies, such as insulation, have been important. The electrification of the U.S. economy has also been associated with declining energy-to-GDP ratios and increased net productivity of all factor inputs. The production and distribution of electricity itself result in a loss of as much as two-thirds of the heat content of the primary energy input; however, the productive efficiency of electrical equipment and processes is thought to compensate for the loss.[8] Also, some believe that the emergence of the idea of conservation as a desirable national goal induced changes in behavior, such as lower thermostat settings.[9]

All major sectors of the economy have shared in the efficiency gains. Efficiency improvements accompanied by a structural shift away from energy-intensive industries have engendered progressively lower energy intensities (energy consumed per unit of value added) in U.S. *industry* (see Figure 12).[10] The *residential* sector

Figure 12

Energy Intensity of U.S. Industry, 1970-90

mtoe/industrial production index

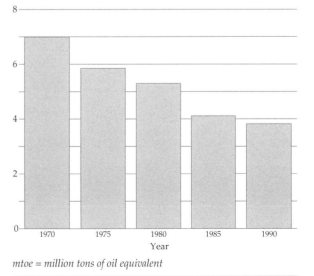

mtoe = million tons of oil equivalent

SOURCE: International Energy Agency and Council of Economic Advisers

experienced a decline in energy consumption per household despite structural factors working the other way, such as increased ownership of major appliances and a greater average heated and lighted floor area. More widespread installation of wall and floor insulation and storm windows in new and existing homes is well documented, as are efficiency improvements in heating equipment and electrical appliances such as refrigerators, air conditioners, and clothes dryers. Developments in the commercial subsector paralleled those in the residential subsector, yielding substantial savings.

Efficiency gains in the transportation sector were particularly large. Despite an increase of 50 percent in the motor vehicle population, gasoline consumption rose only 8 percent between 1973 and 1991, largely because of sharp improvements in auto fuel efficiency. Figure 13 shows that by 1990, 36 percent less fuel was required than in 1973 to cover the total 1973 distance driven.[11]

The prospects for future improvements in energy efficiency are bright, particularly in electric power generation. Although the thermal efficiency of fossil-fueled electric utility plants reached a plateau in the late 1960s (due to a combination of environmental regulations and technological limitations), new processes that push the efficiency of electricity generation up to close to 50 percent (from an average of about 33 percent today) will gradually come on-line. Moreover, some utilities, with the encouragement of regulation, have shifted emphasis from building additional capacity to programs that reduce demand for electricity by promoting conservation. (For a discussion of electric utility conservation programs, see Chapter 4).

PRODUCTION AND PRICES

Figure 14 shows U.S. energy production trends. The gap between domestic energy production and consumption is widening, causing an increasing proportion of total domestic demand to be met by imports. The Department of Energy expects the current shortfall of 16 percent of total consumption to increase to about 21 percent by the year 2010.[12]

FOSSIL FUELS

Coal. Since World War II, coal, oil, and natural gas have each had a turn at being the dominant domestically produced fuel. When productivity and output in the oil and natural gas industries declined during the latter half of the 1980s, coal gained the premier spot. Unless new environmental constraints are adopted, coal is expected to further increase its share of energy production into the 21st century (see Figure 14). U.S. coal reserves account for about 23 percent of the world's total, which is enough to sustain production at the 1991 level for about 270 years. Coal already accounts for 55 percent of the electricity generated by utilities in the United States (see Table 1). If the more optimistic projections for gains in energy efficiency are not fulfilled, demand for electricity may grow strongly both in the United States and abroad. Thus, there will be domestic and export markets for coal.[13] However, the rising concern about global climate change may adversely affect long-run demand because coal's carbon content is higher than

---

Figure 13

U.S. Passenger Car Fuel Consumption and Efficiency, 1966-90

Billions of gallons

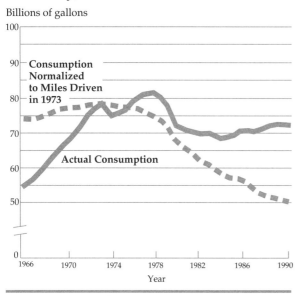

SOURCE: Calculated from Energy Information Administration data

that of other fossil fuels. The coal industry's productivity has been enhanced by a geographic shift of emphasis in mining operations from east of the Mississippi to west of it, where surface mining is more prevalent.[14] Western states, which accounted for only 5 percent of production in 1965, supplied 41 percent of the total in 1991. The shift to western coal has also been encouraged by greater prevalence in the West of more environmentally friendly low-sulphur coal.

Oil and Natural Gas. * Excess capacity in the domestic petroleum industry that existed in the 1950s and 1960s was eliminated in the 1970s as productivity from wells in the lower 48 states declined while demand escalated. Increased production in Alaska temporarily reversed the decline that occurred between 1970 and 1976. However, finding new reserves abroad is cheaper; and since 1986, persistently low oil prices, declining productivity of existing wells, diminishing reserves, and environmental restrictions on access to potential fields have caused domestic output to fall again. There is

general agreement among energy analysts that only the rate of decline in domestic production (not the fact of decline) is in doubt and that U.S. dependence on imported oil is likely to rise rapidly, perhaps to about 60 percent by 2010.[15]

Any forecast of future energy prices is, of course, fraught with uncertainty. However, worldwide oil supplies look quite adequate for the near term if there are no disruptions arising from further political upheavals. Some observers expect that the restoration of Kuwaiti and Iraqi oil production, on top of expanded production in Saudi Arabia and other exporting countries, will dampen price levels over the next few years. Increased efforts from the states of the former Soviet Union may help stabilize prices for the longer term. Nevertheless, some analysts expect that rising demand and the leveling off of production in non-OPEC countries by the end of the decade could push prices up again. If prices do rise, the reliance of the industrialized countries on OPEC will be accentuated. The world's proved reserves-to-production ratio (R/P),[16] which is now esti-

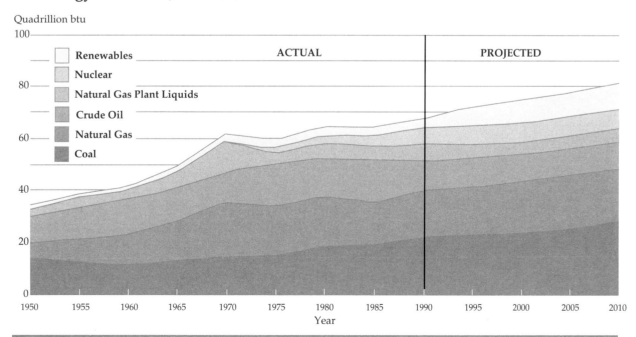

Figure 14

U.S. Energy Production, 1950-2010

Quadrillion btu

Legend:
- Renewables
- Nuclear
- Natural Gas Plant Liquids
- Crude Oil
- Natural Gas
- Coal

ACTUAL | PROJECTED

Year

SOURCE: Energy Information Administration

*See memorandum by ROCCO C. SICILIANO (page 94).

19

mated at about 43 years, has risen by about 25 percent since the mid-1960s. But two-thirds of the world's known reserves are located in the Middle East; and the substantial increase in reserves since 1986, from 700 billion barrels to 1 trillion barrels, results almost exclusively from discoveries in that region, mostly in Saudi Arabia.

If the world market for oil holds prices close to 1992 levels, as many expect, the short- and medium-term market prices of U.S. gasoline (including motor fuel taxes) — already the lowest among the major industrialized countries (see Figure 15) — may not rise to a level that would strongly encourage the development of alternative fuels, induce consumers to buy more fuel-efficient cars, or encourage conservation to any large extent. But concern about air quality and conservation and resulting legislation may have that effect.

Natural gas production in the United States peaked in 1971, then eased due to weak demand. After that, rising prices, government regulation,[17] and uncertainties over supply caused electric utilities and industrial users to move away from gas. However, a revival in industrial consumption buoyed demand in the latter half of the 1980s, and consumption is expected to grow at least over the next decade as electric utilities move toward increased use of combined-cycle generating plants. Uncertainty about future prices is the main reason for some variation in forecasts of domestic natural gas production. Many of the world's natural gas reserves are in the Middle East (31 percent) and the former Soviet Union (40 percent) and cannot be transported cheaply to the United States.[18] Although North America as a whole has large reserves and most analysts agree that imports from Canada may become a more important supplement to U.S. production, they are not expected to become a major source of energy in the United States.

NUCLEAR, RENEWABLE, AND OTHER ENERGY SOURCES

Nuclear power has doubled its share of U.S. electricity generation since 1980 and now accounts for about 22 percent. The United States produces more nuclear power than any other country. But no new plants have been ordered since 1978, and the contribution of nuclear energy will decline unless its political and economic viability can be restored to the point where the operating licenses of existing plants are routinely extended and/or new plants are built. The problems are both systemic and technological. For example, although advances in passive safety systems and standardized plant designs may reduce safety concerns, a number of problems relating to regulation, licensing, and operation will need to be resolved to make nuclear power economically viable. Public anxiety about nuclear power is further accentuated by failure to resolve the question of how to dispose of high-level nuclear waste. However, advocates point out that unlike fossil fuels, nuclear power does not produce carbon dioxide and local air pollutants in the generation of electricity. (For a detailed discussion of these issues, see Chapter 4.)

The situation in other OECD countries is more positive. In March 1991, the governments

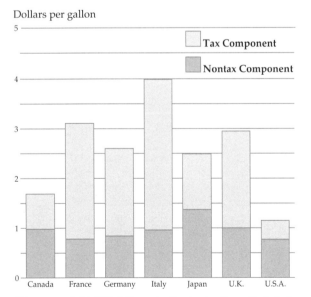

Figure 15

Gasoline Prices in Major Industrialized Countries, 1991

Dollars per gallon

Prices converted to U.S. dollars using Purchasing Power Parity Index

SOURCE: International Energy Agency

of Britain, France, Germany, and Belgium reaffirmed their commitment to nuclear power and to cooperation in the development of new reactors. France now gets 75 percent of its electricity from nuclear power, Belgium 60 percent, Germany 28 percent, and Britain 20 percent. Japan derives 27 percent of its electricity from that source.[19]

Elsewhere in the world, the record on nuclear power is mixed. The large capital cost discourages the building of nuclear plants in developing countries, and the safety of some nuclear reactors in Eastern Europe is of major concern.

Renewable energy currently accounts for about 10 percent of U.S. electricity production. Of this, 9 percent is in the form of hydroelectricity; the remainder comes mostly from solar, municipal waste, wind, and geothermal sources. By improving efficiency and lowering costs, some progress has been made during the past decade in bringing different forms of renewable energy closer to large-scale commercialization. However, many renewable sources are still prohibitively expensive,[20] and there are also problems with variability of access, uncertainty about the extent of resources, and regulation.[21]

Alternative fuels for motor vehicles first attracted great interest (and federal money) during the 1970s as an option for freeing the United States from its dependence on foreign oil. With the calming of oil markets in the 1980s, the alternative fuels programs were promptly forgotten, but they have received renewed attention in the past few years with the growth of environmental concerns. Although reduction of local air pollution is a major consideration in the development of these fuels, their net effect on the atmosphere is unresolved, and most alternative fuels are currently expensive to produce. In addition, there is little physical or regulatory infrastructure for these fuels, and there are questions about vehicle performance.[22] In some cases, for example, the fuel range is inferior to that of gasoline, and improvement in performance involves trade-offs that vitiate positive environmental effects. Consumer acceptance under these circumstances is at best highly uncertain.

TRENDS IN AIR POLLUTION

Poor air quality substantially diminishes the well-being of residents of many regions of the world. Most advanced industrial nations have made progress in reducing air pollution, though air quality is still poor in parts of these countries. But residents of developing countries, as well as Eastern Europe and the former Soviet Union, are frequently subjected to high levels of pollution that exceed World Health Organization (WHO) guidelines (see Figure 16).[23]

It is well established that high levels of air pollution are associated with increased health problems in the exposed population.[24] The severity of the effects depends on the type, duration, and concentration of the pollutant. For example, particulate matter is associated with respiratory distress, while carbon monoxide may be associated with cardiac distress.

Air quality should be thought of not as one issue, but rather as several distinct problems defined by different geographic impacts. Thus,

Figure 16

Average Number of Days Per Year that Concentration of Particulate or Sulphur Dioxide Exceeds WHO Guidelines in Selected Cities

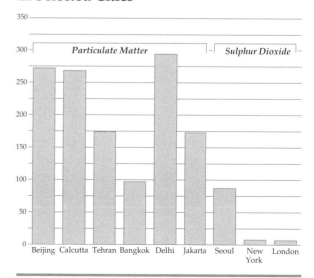

SOURCE: UN Environment Programme and World Health Organization

air quality problems can be local, regional, or global. Often the adverse effects are geographically quite localized, as in the case of urban smog. However, acid deposition, which occurs when pollutants travel hundred of miles from their source and undergo chemical reactions, is generally a regional problem. Finally, there are global issues, such as climate change.

In the sections that follow, we examine national trends in air quality and emissions of pollutants. We discuss local, regional, and global problems separately because their economic, political, and jurisdictional implications are so distinct. However, these problems often have overlapping causes, and it is important that the policy responses for dealing with them be coordinated.

NATIONAL TRENDS IN POLLUTANT EMISSIONS AND AIR QUALITY

In the United States, air pollution was originally recognized as a local public policy problem. The federal government first entered the picture in 1955, with the passage of the Air Pollution Control Act. National goals for air quality were first established in 1963, when the original Clean Air Act was enacted. The 1970 Amendments to the Clean Air Act empowered the EPA to set federal standards for air quality, which were put in place in the 1970s. In recent years, the EPA has promulgated National Ambient Air Quality Standards (NAAQS) for six common pollutants: particulate matter (PM-10, formerly TSP), sulphur dioxide (SO_2), carbon monoxide (CO), nitrogen dioxide (NO_2), tropospheric ozone (O_3), and lead (Pb).

The NAAQS represent the maximum permissible concentrations of these common air pollutants consistent with protecting human health.[25] Congress directed that these standards be uniform across the country and that they provide an adequate margin of safety to protect the public from "any known or anticipated adverse effects" associated with air pollution. Given that some people are sensitive to very small concentrations of pollutants, critics of this approach point out that the margin-of-safety provision may require an unattainable zero level of pollution. They also argue

that it is a serious mistake to set standards without regard to costs of attainment.[26] (For a detailed discussion of these issues, see Chapter 3.)

Substantial reductions in emissions and in national ambient concentrations have been achieved for most of these pollutants since the mid-1970s (see Table 2).[27] In most cases, the decline in emissions is a reversal of long upward trends, suggesting that environmental regulations have had a significant effect (see Figures 17 to 22).[28] An exception is ambient air concentrations of particulate matter, which have been declining since the 1950s. Improvements in air quality in the United States appear to be at least comparable with those made in Japan and Europe.[29]

Although declines were generally quite large in the 1970s, recent data gathered from EPA monitoring show continued reductions in the

Table 2

Recent Decline in Emissions and Ambient Air Concentrations of Pollutants in the United States (percent)

Emissions	1970-80	1980-91	1990-91
Particulate	-52	-18	0
Sulphur oxides	-20	-9	-2
Carbon monoxide	-19	-38	-8
Nitrogen oxides	+24	-20	-3
VOCs [a]	-21	-22	-4
Lead	-66	-93	-3

Concentrations	1975-82	1982-91	1990-91
Particulate	-15	-3[b]	-3[c]
Sulphur dioxide	-33	-20	-4
Carbon monoxide	-31	-30	-5
Nitrogen dioxide	0	-6	0
Ozone	-18	-8	+1
Lead	-64	-89	-18

(a) Volatile organic compounds, a factor in ozone formation
(b) 1982-90
(c) 1989-90

SOURCE: Environmental Protection Agency

U.S. EMISSION TRENDS, 1950-91

Volatile Organic Compounds

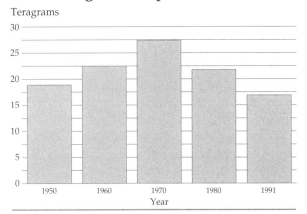

Lead

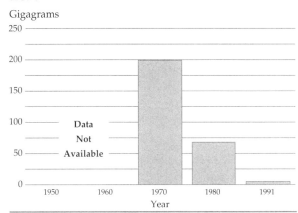

Particulate

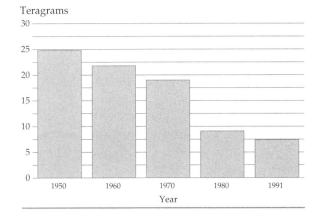

Sulphur Oxides

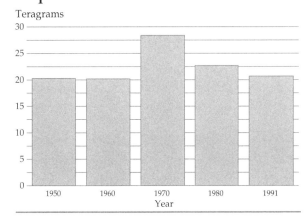

Nitrogen Oxides

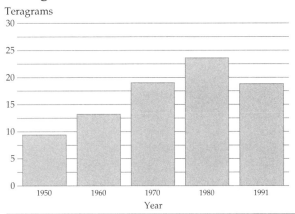

Carbon Monoxide

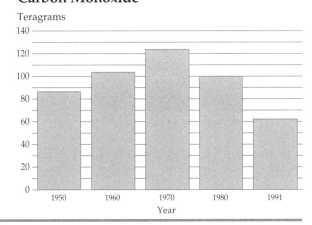

SOURCE: Environmental Protection Agency

23

emission of pollutants and improvement in national air quality in the 1980s and early 1990s.[30] According to EPA measurements, national *concentrations* of SO_2, CO, and O_3 declined 20, 30, and 8 percent respectively during the 10-year period ending in 1991. Concentrations of lead in the air declined 89 percent. This improvement reflects more efficient energy use, changing energy sources (such as the switch to low-sulphur coal and unleaded gasoline), and emission controls.

The major sources of these pollutants are stationary-source fuel combustion (largely electric utilities), transportation, and industrial processes (see Figures 23 to 34). The relative contribution from each source has changed significantly during the last few decades. For example, the contribution from transport (principally motor vehicles) to CO, nitrogen oxides (NO_x), and volatile organic compounds (VOCs) has declined; in fact, industrial processes have overtaken motor vehicles as the largest source of man-made emissions of VOCs.

In absolute terms, emissions of VOCs (precursors of urban ozone) and CO from motor vehicles declined nationally by 38 and 41 percent respectively from 1980 to 1990, according to the EPA, despite a 37 percent increase in vehicle miles travelled.[31] Available data indicate that the decline is continuing.[32] The switch to unleaded gasoline in catalytic converter-equipped cars and the reduced lead content of leaded gasoline brought about a 97 percent decline in lead emissions from transportation sources between 1982 and 1991.[33]

Improvements in efficiency of energy use were also important. The increase in gasoline prices in the 1970s and higher mileage requirements (corporate average fuel economy, or CAFE standards, discussed in Chapter 4) stimulated a sharp improvement in motor vehicle efficiency, which helped to reduce CO_2 emissions. However, the combination of improved efficiency and lower gasoline prices has reduced the cost of driving. As a result, total miles travelled have been rising more rapidly recently and have offset some of the benefits of more fuel-efficient automobiles.

It is important to note that the emissions contribution from vehicles made before 1981 (30 percent of passenger cars on the road in 1990) is greatly out of proportion to their number in the total fleet.[34] As these cars are retired, significant emissions benefits will occur.

Reductions in emissions from sources other than autos were also significant. Sulphur emissions have declined 9 percent since 1980. Almost two-thirds of sulphur emissions are produced by the generation of electricity at coal-fired plants.[35] Nitrogen oxide emissions, which result almost entirely from fuel combustion and motor vehicles, declined 20 percent.[36]

URBAN AIR POLLUTION

Although the United States has made important progress in reducing emissions and improving national air quality, local air quality often fails to meet EPA standards. This is not to say that there has been no progress in urban areas. Most regions meet the air quality standards for NO_2 and lead, and nearly all monitors in urban areas meet EPA SO_2 standards.[37] But in August 1990, the EPA listed 96 areas that failed to meet ozone NAAQS for the years 1987 to 1989 and 41 areas that failed to meet carbon monoxide NAAQS in the 1988-1989 period. This urban pollution problem was an important factor in the passage of the 1990 Amendments to the Clean Air Act. When the EPA completed its review of ozone and carbon monoxide data for the 1989-1991 period, the number of areas that did not meet the national standard for ozone declined to 56, and the number for carbon monoxide dropped to 29.[38]

Many of the 90 largest metropolitan statistical areas (MSAs) in the continental United States failed to meet EPA standards for one or more pollutants. Table 3 (page 27) shows the number of areas for each pollutant in 1991. The most pervasive problem continues to be tropospheric ozone, which is the most prevalent photochemical oxidant and an important component of urban smog. A recent study by the National Research Council concluded that efforts to reduce urban ozone have failed largely because of inaccurate measurement and control of emissions and inadequate understanding

SOURCES OF POLLUTANTS BY END-USE SECTOR, 1970 AND 1991

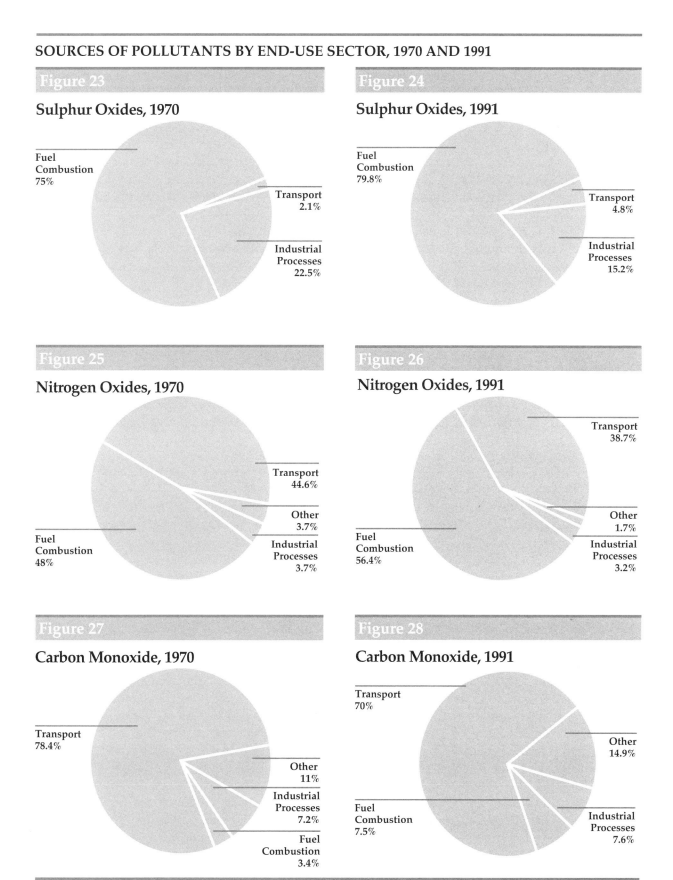

Figure 23

Sulphur Oxides, 1970

Fuel Combustion 75%

Transport 2.1%

Industrial Processes 22.5%

Figure 24

Sulphur Oxides, 1991

Fuel Combustion 79.8%

Transport 4.8%

Industrial Processes 15.2%

Figure 25

Nitrogen Oxides, 1970

Transport 44.6%

Other 3.7%

Fuel Combustion 48%

Industrial Processes 3.7%

Figure 26

Nitrogen Oxides, 1991

Transport 38.7%

Other 1.7%

Fuel Combustion 56.4%

Industrial Processes 3.2%

Figure 27

Carbon Monoxide, 1970

Transport 78.4%

Other 11%

Industrial Processes 7.2%

Fuel Combustion 3.4%

Figure 28

Carbon Monoxide, 1991

Transport 70%

Other 14.9%

Fuel Combustion 7.5%

Industrial Processes 7.6%

SOURCE: Environmental Protection Agency

SOURCES OF POLLUTANTS BY END-USE SECTOR, 1970 AND 1991

Figure 29

Volatile Organic Compounds, 1970

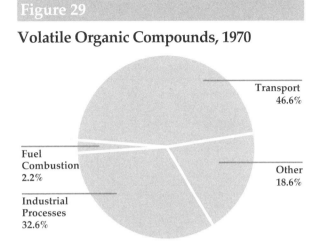

Transport
46.6%

Fuel
Combustion
2.2%

Industrial
Processes
32.6%

Other
18.6%

Figure 30

Volatile Organic Compounds, 1991

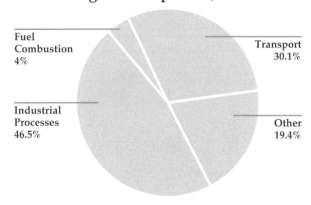

Fuel
Combustion
4%

Transport
30.1%

Industrial
Processes
46.5%

Other
19.4%

Figure 31

Lead, 1970

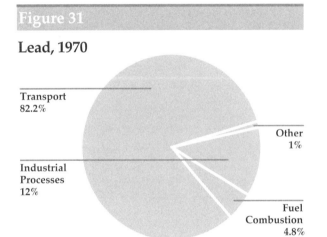

Transport
82.2%

Industrial
Processes
12%

Other
1%

Fuel
Combustion
4.8%

Figure 32

Lead, 1991

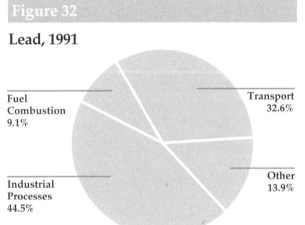

Fuel
Combustion
9.1%

Transport
32.6%

Industrial
Processes
44.5%

Other
13.9%

Figure 33

Particulate, 1970

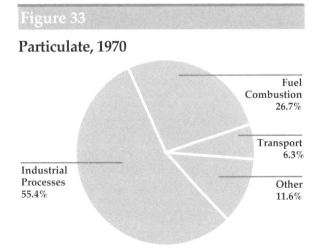

Fuel
Combustion
26.7%

Transport
6.3%

Industrial
Processes
55.4%

Other
11.6%

Figure 34

Particulate, 1991

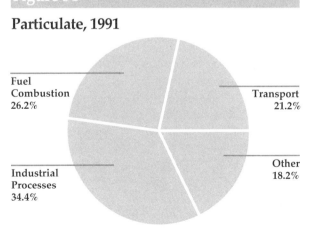

Fuel
Combustion
26.2%

Transport
21.2%

Industrial
Processes
34.4%

Other
18.2%

SOURCE: Environmental Protection Agency

Table 3

Number of Large Metropolitan Statistical Areas Failing to Meet Air Quality Standards, 1991

Pollutant	Number of MSAs
PM-10 [a]	7
Sulphur dioxide [a]	0
Carbon monoxide	10
Nitrogen dioxide	1
Ozone	38
Lead	9

(a) Annual arithmetic mean.

SOURCE: Environmental Protection Agency

of the relative effectiveness of VOC and NO_x controls. The study recommended a fundamental change in the strategy used to eliminate ozone in many geographic areas.[39]

The EPA's summary index of air quality, the Pollutant Standards Index (PSI), for 15 major urban areas shows considerable variation among cities and in different years for the same city. Los Angeles clearly has the most serious and persistent problem among this country's major urban areas;[40] the PSI exceeded 100 (the unhealthy range) on more than 200 days a year during 1988 and 1989 (see Table 4, page 28). No other major urban area experienced a PSI in this unhealthy range for more than 48 days in either 1988 or 1989. In 1991, the 15 major urban areas experienced a cumulative 285 days of PSI above 100; but Los Angeles accounted for 156, or 55 percent, of those days.

Although two-thirds of the U.S. population live in areas that meet federal standards for all pollutants, according to EPA estimates, 86.4 million people resided in counties that did not meet the air quality standard for one or more pollutants on more than one day during 1991 (see Figure 35, page 29). The pollutants affecting the greatest number of people were ozone (69.7 million people), carbon monoxide (19.9 million), and particulate matter (21.5 million). Given the major sources of common pollutants (industrial processes and motor vehicles), most of these people are likely to be living in densely populated urban areas.

The average decline in national ambient concentration levels of the pollutants subject to NAAQS (other than lead, which fell sharply) was about 13 percent in the last decade. Many analysts find this rate of progress disappointing, particularly when so many areas do not meet EPA standards. At the same time, however, it must be recognized that the cost of removing increasingly smaller amounts of pollutants rose. Moreover, the improvement in national air quality occurred during a period when total output (real GNP) and industrial production grew about 29 percent. Thus, for the nation as a whole, the emission of pollutants per unit of output showed considerable improvement (see Table 5, page 29).

ACID DEPOSITION: A REGIONAL PROBLEM

Although adverse effects on human health are the most important consequence of air pollution, the acid effect of pollution is also a concern because of its impact on the nation's forests, lakes, and agriculture. (The acid effect is popularly referred to as *acid rain*, even though acidic substances fall not only as rain but also as dry particles, gases, snow, fog, and dew.) Acid deposition is the end of a complex process that begins with the emission of such chemicals as SO_2, NO_x, and VOCs; these substances are transformed in the atmosphere into acid. Man-made emissions play a far greater role than natural emissions, except in the case of VOCs. The largest man-made source is SO_2 resulting from the combustion of fossil fuels, especially coal, by electric utilities and industry. Although damage from acid rain has been reported by environmentalists and government authorities,[41] there is still considerable debate about the acid process, the consequences of acid deposition, and the benefits of regulation relative to the costs.[42]

Because of the use of tall stacks to disperse emissions from plant areas, the acid-causing pollutants often travel in the atmosphere for hundreds of miles, frequently across state and

27

Table 4

Number of Days Pollutant Standards Index Exceeded 100, 1980-91

	1980	1981	1982	1983	1984	1985	1986	1987	1988	1989	1990	1991	Average Annual Change 80/81 to 90/91
Atlanta	7	9	5	23	8	9	17	19	15	3	16	5	0.25
Boston	8	2	5	16	7	3	2	5	12	2	1	3	-0.30
Chicago	34	3	3	16	8	6	4	10	18	2	3	8	-1.30
Dallas	10	12	12	18	11	15	5	8	3	3	5	0	-0.85
Denver	35	51	52	67	61	38	45	36	18	11	7	7	-3.60
Detroit	–	18	19	18	7	2	6	9	17	12	3	7	-1.30
Houston	10	34	49	70	48	47	44	54	48	32	48	39	2.15
Kansas City	13	7	0	4	12	4	8	6	3	2	2	1	-0.85
Los Angeles	220	228	195	184	208	196	210	187	226	212	164	156	-6.40
New York	119	100	69	62	110	60	53	40	41	10	12	16	-9.55
Philadelphia	52	29	44	56	31	25	21	36	34	19	11	24	-2.30
Pittsburgh	20	17	13	33	15	5	6	14	26	11	11	3	-1.15
San Francisco	2	1	2	4	2	5	4	1	1	0	1	0	-0.10
Seattle	33	42	19	19	4	26	18	13	8	4	2	0	-3.65
Washington	38	23	25	53	30	15	11	23	34	7	5	16	-2.00
TOTAL	601	558	512	643	562	456	454	461	504	330	273	285	-30.05

Pollutant Standards Index Time Trend Lines, Selected Cities

Days per year

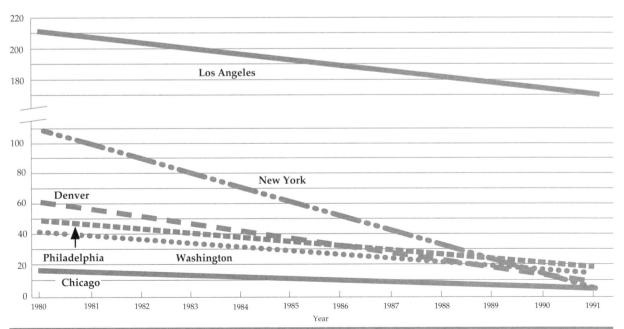

SOURCE: Environmental Protection Agency

Figure 35

Number of People in United States Living in Counties Not Meeting National Air Quality Standards for Different Pollutants, 1991

Pollutant

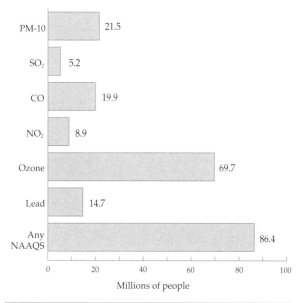

Millions of people

SOURCE: Environmental Protection Agency

Table 5

Emissions Intensity, 1981 and 1991
Ratio of teragrams per year of emissions to trillions of 1987 dollars of output

	1981	1991
Particulate matter	**2.23**	**1.54**
Sulphur oxides	**5.86**	**4.30**
Nitrogen oxides	**5.55**	**3.89**
VOCs	**5.52**	**3.50**
Carbon monoxide	**25.51**	**12.88**
Lead [a]	**13.90**	**1.03**

(a) Gigagrams per year/trillions of 1987 dollars

SOURCES: Environmental Protection Agency and Council of Economic Advisers

even national boundaries. Thus, states in the East and Canada have complained about emissions from plants in the Midwest. This situation has made it difficult to achieve political agreement on how to share the costs of reducing acid-causing emissions. But a compromise was struck in the 1990 Amendments to the Clean Air Act that is expected to significantly reduce these emissions over the next decade.

CLIMATE CHANGE: A GLOBAL ISSUE

In addition to seasonal and year-to-year fluctuations in temperature and precipitation, various fluctuations in the earth's climate that occur over longer periods, ranging from about 10 years to many thousands of years, are well documented. In this century, there have been several periods of sustained rising and falling temperatures, the cause of which is not fully resolved. Today, some scientists believe that the earth may have entered a warming period initiated by human activities that cause rising concentrations of certain GHGs in the atmosphere.

It has long been understood that water vapor, carbon dioxide, and several other gases that occur naturally in the atmosphere permit sunlight to reach and warm the earth's surface while keeping the heat from escaping back into space. Without this natural *greenhouse effect*, the earth would be too cold for habitation. For perhaps a hundred years, scientists have also recognized that certain human activities, such as the burning of fossil fuels, might enhance the greenhouse effect by increasing emissions of GHGs such as CO_2 into the atmosphere.

It is also well documented that man-made emissions of these gases have risen rapidly in this century. Great efforts have been made to identify the causes and effects of these emissions. In 1988, the United Nations Environment Programme (UNEP) and the World Meteorological Organization (WMO) formed a study group of scientists, economists, and policy makers called the Intergovernmental Panel on Climate Change (IPCC), which undertook a two-year assessment of the available scientific research on climate change. The IPCC report, issued in August 1990, identified several aspects of the greenhouse effect that are understood with some degree of certainty and several other issues that are not settled.[43] These findings were largely confirmed in an update issued in January 1992.[44]

Scientists generally agree that water vapor, principally from natural sources, is the largest contributor to the greenhouse effect. There are a number of other important naturally occurring GHGs, including carbon dioxide, methane, and ozone. Small particulates in the atmosphere resulting from events such as volcanic eruptions can also affect climate. In its 1990 report, the IPCC found that the key GHGs influenced by human activity are carbon dioxide (CO_2), methane (CH_4), chlorofluorocarbons (CFC-11 and CFC-12), nitrous oxide (N_2O), and ozone (O_3). As explained below, however, the greenhouse role of CFCs is now less certain. Human activities that increase emissions of these gases include burning fossil fuels (coal, oil, natural gas), deforestation, fertilization of croplands, and cattle rearing. The relative contributions of industrialized and developing nations to greenhouse gas emissions are shown

in Figure 36. In industrial countries, the greenhouse emissions are produced mostly by energy use, whereas in developing countries, the main causes are deforestation and agricultural activities. But this situation is changing. The OECD estimates that CO_2 emissions from energy-related sources will increase by 2.3 percent a year for the world, 1.2 percent a year in OECD countries, and 3.7 percent a year in developing countries through 2005, assuming that oil prices rise to $30 per barrel in real terms by 2001.

Largely because of the growth of industry and the improvement of living standards, CO_2 emissions have risen over the past hundred years. The atmospheric concentration of CO_2 is estimated to have increased by about 25 percent from preindustrial levels and to be rising currently at a rate of about 0.5 percent a year. Table 6 shows widely used estimates of GHG concentrations. Carbon dioxide, which stays in the atmosphere for decades and perhaps even centuries after release, is believed to account for about 55 percent of the warming potential produced by human activity at the present time, and its share is expected to rise along with

Figure 36

Regional Greenhouse Gas Emissions as a Percent of World Total

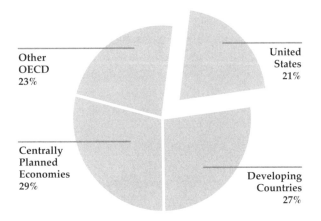

Other OECD 23%

United States 21%

Centrally Planned Economies 29%

Developing Countries 27%

Estimates are for 1985

SOURCE: Office of Technology Assessment

Figure 37

U. S. CO_2 Emissions by Sector as a Percent of U.S. Total, 1988

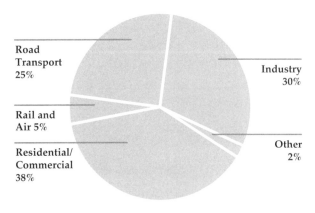

Road Transport 25%

Industry 30%

Rail and Air 5%

Residential/ Commercial 38%

Other 2%

SOURCE: International Energy Agency

energy consumption. However, the dispersion of CO_2 emissions is not well understood. This led the authors of a major study by the National Academy of Sciences to conclude that "until the redistribution of newly emitted CO_2 is more thoroughly understood, reliable projections of the rate of increase of atmospheric CO_2 will lack credibility even for precisely estimated emission rates."[45] CO_2 is produced by a wide range of basic economic activities. Sectoral contributions to emissions of CO_2 in the United States are shown in Figure 37.

Methane is an important GHG produced by such human activities as rice production, cattle rearing, biomass burning, coal mining, and natural gas field operations; it now accounts for about 20 percent of the greenhouse effect. Methane does not remain in the atmosphere for long. Nevertheless, atmospheric concentrations have doubled in the last century and are believed to be growing at an annual rate of 0.9 percent. Each molecule of this gas has about 25 times the warming effect of CO_2. On the other hand, nitrous oxide concentrations, which

appear to be produced by agricultural activity (perhaps soil bacteria action with nitrogen fertilizers), are estimated to have increased by only 8 percent since preindustrial times and are growing slowly. According to the 1990 IPCC report, CFCs, which do not occur in nature, have an enormous warming effect and a long life. More recently, scientists have cast doubt on the greenhouse effects of CFCs.

CFCs are manufactured for a number of uses, including solvents, refrigeration, air conditioning, and industrial processing. However, they are expected to be gradually replaced by other chemicals. In 1987, a decline in the stratospheric ozone layer, which shields the earth from harmful ultraviolet radiation, was observed in the Antarctic region. The primary cause of the ozone depletion was thought to be the release of CFCs into the atmosphere. In September 1987, 47 nations reached an agreement, the Montreal Protocol on Substances that Deplete the Ozone Layer, which is intended to phase out CFC production.[46] The United States initially counted the reduction in CFCs as part

Table 6

IPCC 1990 Estimates for Principal Greenhouse Gases Influenced by Human Activity

	CO_2	CH_4	CFC-11[a]	CFC-12[a]	N_2O
Preindustrial atmospheric concentration	280 ppmv	0.8 ppmv	0	0	288 ppbv
1990 atmospheric concentration	353 ppmv	1.72 ppmv	280 pptv	484 pptv	310 ppbv
Current rate of annual atmospheric accumulation	1.8 ppmv (0.5%)	0.015 ppmv (0.9%)	9.5 pptv (4%)	17 pptv (4%)	0.8 ppbv (0.25%)
Atmospheric lifetime[b] (years)	50 - 200	10	65	130	150

NOTE: ppmv = parts per million by volume; ppbv = parts per billion by volume; pptv = parts per trillion by volume.

(a) More recent evidence suggests that the overall radiative effects of increased CFC concentrations may be neutralized by the ozone stripping impact of these gases because stratospheric ozone is also a greenhouse gas.

(b) Except for CO_2, this is defined as the ratio of the atmospheric concentration to the total rate of removal. For CO_2, it is the approximate time needed for the CO_2 concentration to adjust to changes in emissions.

SOURCE: World Meteorological Organization. For additional information, see National Academy of Sciences, *Policy Implications of Greenhouse Warming*, p.11.

of its contribution to reducing greenhouse gas emissions. But a study prepared by scientists organized by the United Nations Environment Programme recently observed that the emission of CFCs may result in a net decrease in warming potential. This is because stratospheric ozone, which is depleted by CFCs, is also a greenhouse gas.[47]

Emissions of GHGs are expected to grow during the next several decades, largely because energy use is expected to rise with population growth and economic development. It has been estimated that preindustrial concentrations of CO_2 will approximately double by about 2025 if current trends continue. Many scientists, including two eminent groups — the IPCC and the U.S. National Academy of Sciences (NAS) — have concluded that global temperatures are likely to rise gradually as a result of such an increase in greenhouse gases. The IPCC estimates that the realized global mean atmospheric temperature could rise by about 0.3° centigrade per decade. Because ocean temperatures rise slowly, the exchange of heat between the ocean and the atmosphere will delay the full effect for decades. The IPCC update issued in January 1992 concluded that "the evidence from modeling studies, from observations and sensitivity analyses indicate that the sensitivity of global mean surface temperatures to doubling CO_2 is unlikely to lie outside of 1.5° to 4.5° centigrade."[48] Such a rise in temperatures could have numerous adverse impacts, according to these scientists, including a rise in sea levels (NAS says the rise in sea levels could be zero to 24 inches), changed ocean currents, more frequent storms, and substantial changes in regional temperatures and precipitation. However, increased CO_2 and global warming could also have positive effects, such as increased plant growth, and temperatures and rainfall might be more conducive to habitation in some parts of the world.

The IPCC estimates that a 0.3° to 0.6° centigrade rise in mean surface air temperatures has occurred over the last century, an amount that "is broadly consistent with predictions of climate models" but "could be largely due to . . . natural variability."[49] Users of the climate models concede many shortcomings. By necessity, such models include oversimplified representations of oceans, clouds, the biosphere, and other critical elements of climate change. Nevertheless, many analysts believe that they provide strong evidence for global warming. However, there are critics who are very doubtful that the currently available mathematical models can provide useful predictions.[50] The question of the models' accuracy cannot easily be resolved by historical data because natural events, such as volcanic eruptions, can have relatively significant effects that may mask the effects of GHGs. Some scientists believe that increased cloud cover or greater absorption of GHGs, which in itself may not be benign, could have the positive effect of mitigating the impact of these gases on temperatures. Others, however, fear that climate models underestimate warming because of feedback effects that could cause global warming to become an increasingly severe problem, once started. For example, as air warms, concentrations of water vapor (a GHG) could rise, thereby intensifying the greenhouse effect. On the other hand, some of this water vapor could condense into clouds and create a cooling effect.

Scientific research is not expected to resolve many of these issues for a decade or more. In the meantime, the consensus of the scientific community is unchanged: With a considerable time lag, the ongoing increase in GHG concentrations could have a significant effect on the earth's climate, including a rise in average global temperatures. It is generally agreed, however, that there is a great deal of uncertainty about: (1) the *magnitude* of the changes in the earth's climate, given a projection of greenhouse emissions, (2) the regional effects on climate, and (3) the effects on the ecology.

There is also considerable uncertainty about the social and economic effects of global climate change. Modern societies have demonstrated their ability to succeed in a wide variety of climates, with far more variability in temperatures than is likely to be produced by the greenhouse effect. A recent study of potential economic effects pointed out that in economies such as that of the United States, where only a small part of national output originates in climate-sensitive sectors, the impact on incomes of a rise in temperatures such as that suggested by the IPCC should be quite small.[51] But the impact on developing countries, which depend much more heavily on outdoor economic activity, could be quite serious.

The uncertainty about global climate change has divided both scientists and environmentalists on the question of appropriate public policy. Some counsel postponing costly action that would limit GHG emissions until research yields more information about their effects. Others favor quick action, citing the persistence of GHGs in the atmosphere and the lagged effect on climate to argue that action must be taken long before there are measurable effects. These issues and their implications for policy are discussed in detail in Chapter 4.

The greenhouse effect is truly a global issue that can be addressed successfully only by the cooperation of many nations. Because the emission of GHGs anywhere in the world affects the entire atmosphere, no nation can isolate itself from the potential consequences of increases in another nation's emissions. Moreover, no single nation's actions can have a decisive impact on the greenhouse effect. Even the United States, which accounts for nearly 20 percent of CO_2 emissions, cannot *by itself* have a major influence on atmospheric concentrations of GHGs without accepting a crippling cost burden *and* running the risk that offsetting increases in emissions by other countries could nullify the benefits. In any case, the U.S. share of CO_2 emissions is already declining, as are those of other developed countries.[52] By contrast, CO_2 emissions are rising in developing countries because of economic gains and because they tend to be inefficient users of energy.[53]

Chapter 3

PRINCIPLES OF SOUND REGULATION

The improvement of environmental quality is now an accepted priority in the United States. Federal legislation passed during the last three decades has committed the nation to the goal of environmental protection, and the quality of the environment has improved in recent years in many areas. CED believes that continued progress in environmental protection will determine in considerable measure the quality of life not only for this generation but also for generations to come.

At the same time, our investigations indicate that regulatory policies relating to the environment are in urgent need of reform. Costly command-and-control regulations must be replaced wherever possible by less costly regulations that rely on market mechanisms and benefit-cost analysis. From 1972 to 1990, the cost of environmental protection in the United States increased from 0.9 percent to 2.1 percent of GNP. The direct cost of pollution control reached about $115 billion in 1990 and continues to rise.[1] When fully implemented, the Clean Air Act Amendments of 1990 are expected to add $20 to $30 billion more per year. With economic costs so high, it is imperative that the nation receive the most value from those resources used for environmental purposes. But all too frequently, the cost of environmental standards exceeds their benefits, and the regulatory methods employed to achieve these standards are inefficient. As a consequence, environmental regulations often impose unnecessary compliance costs. A recent study estimated that environmental compliance costs in the 1973-85 period lowered the level of real GNP by about 2.6 percent, or about $150 billion at current levels of GNP.[2] Other analysts have found even larger economic effects.[3] Of course, society also benefits from improvements in environmental conditions, and generally these benefits are not included in GNP. But this does not deny that the adverse economic effects of environmental regulations should be minimized by adopting the most cost-effective means of achieving air quality goals.

In Chapter 4, we recommend specific reforms in several areas of regulatory policy dealing with air quality and energy use. However, before specific changes can be considered, it is important to consider the principles that should underlie regulatory reform. In this chapter, we look at regulatory principles with particular emphasis on three questions: (1) Why is government intervention to protect the environment necessary in a market economy? (2) When policy makers consider goals for the environment, what factors should influence their choice of air quality standards? (3) How can the control mechanisms used by regulatory authorities be made more efficient without sacrificing environmental standards?

In evaluating the relative merits of alternative goals and methods of environmental management, we emphasize economic factors, particularly strategies that maximize the benefits and minimize the costs to society. We also recognize that many noneconomic factors — cultural, ethical, and others — play a legitimate role in environmental policy. However, these issues are beyond the scope of this statement. Moreover, despite our emphasis on economic efficiency, we recognize that the burden of regulation may not fall evenly and that it may be necessary to compensate lower-income individuals when the impact of regulation is regressive.

In the practical world, regional politics are sometimes a major impediment to reform because elected public officials are pressured to minimize the costs to their constituents rather than to enact reforms that lower costs for society as a whole. But these political constraints may weaken; rising costs of environmental protection have begun to encourage politicians to identify regulatory reforms that could lead to improved environmental quality at a lower cost. Politicians may also find it less costly to compensate those who are damaged by regulatory reform than to forego the savings possible from reform.[4]

There are now growing political pressures at the international level for increased regulatory activities to address the issue of global climate change. Limiting emissions of GHGs is potentially very costly, a fact that makes the regulatory reforms we propose even more urgent.

WHY MARKET INTERVENTION IS NEEDED TO CURB AIR POLLUTION

There is ample evidence that countries with nonmarket economic systems have not protected their environment as well as decentralized market economies. At the same time, the experience of advanced industrial societies has shown that when free markets are left to themselves, they do not provide sufficient incentives to ensure environmental quality. The reasons for this "market failure" are easy to understand.

Decentralized, competitive markets provide an incentive for producers to supply the types and amounts of goods and services desired by consumers and to adopt efficient methods of production. For most private goods, market prices encourage an optimal level of output at which the costs to producers and the benefits to consumers are equalized at the margin. Government intervention in markets for such goods would reduce economic efficiency by encouraging the wrong level of output and/or methods of production.

In certain cases, however, free markets are not likely to achieve such an efficient outcome. The extreme case is that of pure public goods, such as national defense. These cannot be provided efficiently in the marketplace because use by one consumer does not exclude use by others, and therefore, sellers cannot easily exclude nonpurchasers from consumption. The existence of natural monopolies is another case where appropriately designed government intervention may improve economic efficiency. This is the basis for many public utility regulations.

Free markets may also be inefficient when economic transactions result in costs or benefits to third parties not involved in the transactions. Because these social costs or benefits (sometimes called *externalities* or *spillovers*) are not reflected in the price, the private market may not generate appropriate levels of output. Pollution resulting from private production is an example of a social cost that is not reflected in the market price. That is, when economic activity leads to pollution, market prices understate the true social cost and therefore do not provide appropriate signals to producers and consumers. As a result, production and consumption of goods that generate pollution exceed efficient levels. When private economic activity causes unacceptable levels of pollution, intervention by regulators is needed to correct this inefficiency.

In principle, the economic inefficiency can be reduced if the external social costs of pollution are "internalized" — that is, included in production costs and price. The resulting increase in production costs would encourage producers to find ways to reduce pollution and discourage consumption of products whose production involves pollution. **CED believes that, as far as possible, environmental regulation should aim to internalize the properly measured external social costs of pollution.***

* See memorandum by EDWIN LUPBERGER (page 94).

It is conceivable that the external costs of pollution could be internalized through the legal system without government regulation.[5] But as a practical matter, the multiplicity of polluters and pollutees makes legal approaches more expensive than government regulation in most cases.

AIR QUALITY GOALS

Given the need for government intervention to reduce pollution, the next question is what standards should be chosen for environmental quality. If zero pollution is not achievable, what level of pollution is acceptable? Is there an optimal level of air pollution? Congress has charged the EPA with establishing standards for ambient air quality (legal ceilings on the allowable outdoor concentrations of a pollutant) and for emissions of certain pollutants. Several approaches have been considered for designing air quality standards.

- The **zero-risk approach** requires regulators to set the air quality standard at a threshold level that would ensure against *any* adverse health or other effects. This approach underlies the EPA's National Ambient Air Quality Standards (NAAQs).

- **Technology-based regulations** permit only that amount of pollution that would remain after installation of the "best available" or similar technology.

- The **net-benefits approach** determines goals by balancing the costs and benefits of environmental protection in order to ensure that the cost of additional protection does not exceed the additional benefit derived from achieving that standard.

Congress and the EPA have generally employed the first two approaches to set air quality standards. A drawback of the zero-risk approach is that the cost of achieving the standard does not receive serious consideration. For example, the EPA is directed by the Clean Air Act to set NAAQs at a level that will provide an "adequate margin of safety" to protect the public from "any known or anticipated adverse effects." This standard fails to confront the trade-offs between the damage caused by pollution and the cost of reducing pollution. This approach also assumes that there is a precise threshold at which air quality becomes harmful to human health. Unfortunately, scientific evidence suggests that there is no such threshold. Some people may be sensitive to even very small amounts of pollution. Thus, the zero-risk standard could not be achieved without shutting down virtually all production, an outcome that society would find intolerable.[6]

Technology-based regulations have been used extensively to set emissions standards.[7] In nonattainment areas, the EPA has employed the "lowest achievable emission rate" (LAER) standard. The "best available control technology" (BACT) has been applied to new sources of emissions in places designated "PSD" areas (PSD stands for "prevention of significant deterioration"). Provisions of the Clean Air Act of 1990 pertaining to hazardous air pollutants require that 189 chemicals be regulated by the "maximum available control technology" (MACT), regardless of the toxicity of the chemical or the number of people exposed.[8] Such standards are unsatisfactory because they do not give sufficient consideration to costs. Moreover, they may discourage the development of a new, lower-cost technology because producers have no incentive to do better than the standard.

BALANCING BENEFITS AND COSTS

There is a growing realization that although benefit-cost analysis is challenging and sometimes controversial, it offers a more rational approach for setting environmental standards. A critical fact of pollution control is that beyond some point, the cost of eliminating an additional unit of emissions tends to rise sharply as the amount of emissions is reduced. At the same time, the incremental benefit generally declines as emissions are reduced. When the cost of tightening standards exceeds the benefit, tighter standards have no net social benefit, assuming costs and benefits have been measured correctly. Both common sense and economics indicate that these factors should be considered in choosing air quality standards. Unfortunately, a major shortcoming of the Clean Air Act as it is currently interpreted is that it prohibits consideration of costs (and consequently the balancing of costs and benefits) for setting ambient air standards.[9] Although many observers believe that costs are considered whenever standards are set, the practice is not openly acknowledged.[10] Moreover, there is no attempt to evaluate costs and benefits in a formal way that would give the public an opportunity to judge the reasonableness of the standards.

The basic approach of benefit-cost analysis is employed by individuals and businesses in everyday activity and is easily understood (see "Benefit-Cost Analysis and Environmental Standards," page 38). As an analytical tool, its principles are well developed and widely accepted.[11] Of course, its application to specific issues is often difficult and requires extensive research. In some cases, the costs of reducing pollution are not easily estimated; the benefits are frequently even more difficult to estimate. The difficulties of measuring benefits reflect uncertainty about the scientific evidence concerning the adverse effects of pollution and about the appropriate valuation to be given to improvements. Frequently, studies that quantify benefits associated with reductions in pollution find it necessary to estimate a wide range of possible benefits, thereby limiting the value of the information. But despite the complexity of the analysis and the fact that the results cannot always be conclusive, a great deal of information can be gained by examining the range of estimates of costs and benefits.

Opposition to this type of analysis is often based on opposition to quantification of certain benefits. Some are unwilling to attach dollar values to improvements in human health and reduced morbidity, though such calculations are frequently made, at least implicitly, in normal human behavior. The value of these calculations is now widely accepted by scholars of many diciplines.[12]

Benefit-cost calculations provide essential information for evaluating air quality standards. Even crude estimates of compliance costs and benefits derived from further reductions in pollution may be sufficient to avoid serious errors in setting standards. It is known that the cost of tightening standards is often very high, but this does not mean that benefit-cost analysis would necessarily lead to more relaxed standards. The benefits of improving environmental quality may be even higher. This can be determined only by an analysis of each standard. **CED recommends adoption of the practice of using information on costs and benefits to set ambient air standards.[13] We believe that every reasonable effort should be made to quantify costs and benefits in order to ensure that pollution control standards are cost-effective.[14]**

UNIFORMITY OF STANDARDS

The EPA standards for ambient air quality are uniform across the nation, though monitoring and enforcement cover only selected areas. It is evident, however, that the gains from achieving ambient air standards, such as improvements in health and reduced damage to buildings, are not uniform. Pollution is a serious threat to the health of more people in congested urban areas than in sparsely populated rural areas.[15] But there are practical reasons, in many cases, for favoring national standards. Some observers fear that if each community set its own pollution standards, competition among regions to attract businesses would make it difficult to ensure basic health standards for all citizens. It is also argued that local standards could lead to unnecessary diversity that would raise manufacturing costs significantly for some products.

Similar considerations apply to emission standards. In some circumstances, applying the same standard to sources in different locations can be a great waste of resources and can cause considerable inequity among regions and economic groups.[16] But the relative merits of national and local emissions standards need to be examined for each regulation. For example,

BENEFIT-COST ANALYSIS AND ENVIRONMENTAL STANDARDS

In their everyday lives, individuals evaluate the advantages and disadvantages of the alternatives available to them and act in a way that gives them the greatest net advantage. When considering new projects, business firms base their decisions on estimates of revenues received (benefits) and payments for inputs (costs). Benefit-cost analysis is simply the application of this principle of rational behavior to the public policy arena; when faced with policy choices, policy makers should consider both the costs and the benefits and carry forward only those projects where benefits exceed costs. The calculation of benefits and costs is more complicated for the public sector than the private sector, however, because the private sector can measure benefits and costs at market prices, whereas the public sector must consider social costs and benefits not reflected in market prices.

It is often easier to estimate the costs than the benefits of environmental regulation. To measure the costs, analysts could gather information on the amount of money spent by individual firms to comply with a specific environmental standard. Or the approach may involve aggregated data on industry inputs. But there is plenty of uncertainty in estimating costs. For example, because of changing technology, it is difficult to estimate future costs.

The benefit of environmental protection is the reduction in damage from pollution. Thus, calculations begin with a damage estimate. To measure the benefits of a proposed air pollution standard, for example, the projected reductions in emissions are converted into estimates of ambient air concentrations. Then studies on the relation between air quality and agriculture output, health, and other factors are used to estimate the extent to which damage to crops is reduced and human health improved. For example, agriculture crop models have been used to estimate the future annual damage to crops from global warming.[a] The dollar cost of damage can frequently be measured using actual or inferred market prices of commodities or other goods and services. Market prices provide an indication of society's willingness to pay for reduced damage. But sometimes valuations must be inferred from other data. For example, to estimate the damage resulting from emissions of hazardous pollutants, public health data on the incidence of disease caused by pollution and data on the cost of treatment might be employed. Of course, it is frequently quite difficult to identify the health effects of air pollution precisely and to quantify the willingness to pay for improved health. Moreover, in some cases, the benefits are intangible, requiring the analyst to make qualitative rather than quantitative estimates.

---

care must be taken to make sure that tailoring standards to local conditions does not discriminate against established producers. **But when there is an opportunity for substantial net gains by adopting standards that vary according to local conditions, regulators should introduce such changes.**

COORDINATING ENVIRONMENTAL AND ECONOMIC GOALS

In setting environmental standards, regulators should be aware of possible conflicts between environmental and other policies. For example, different technology-based emissions standards frequently distinguish between old and new sources of emissions. Section 111 of the Clean Air Act provides more stringent performance standards for new sources. It could

be argued that such distinctions are in some sense equitable because the owners of old sources invested under a different regulatory regime. Grandfathering may be necessary to prevent discrimination against established producers and to decrease uncertainty about future regulations that might otherwise reduce investment. However, studies have shown that distinctions between new and old sources can also discourage investment in new facilities, depending on the particular circumstance.[17] **We believe that regulations should not discourage business from seeking the least-cost method of meeting environmental standards, whether that be modification of existing facilities or construction of new ones.** New- and old-source regulations may also conflict with fiscal policies designed to encourage busi-

Many object to applying benefit-cost analysis to environmental regulation because they believe that it is impossible to objectively evaluate the benefits to society of clean air. Critics also find it morally repugnant to quantify benefits to human health and morbidity. However, it is necessary to recognize that most people implicitly make such estimates in their everyday decisions. For example, when individuals insure their health, or when they decide how much higher the wage must be for a job that involves added risk to life or health, they are providing some indication of how they evaluate life and health. Indeed, information of this sort can be useful in estimating the benefits of a clean environment. Peer review would reduce the tendency to skew data for political purposes and increase confidence in the range of estimates. Furthermore, the fact that there is a degree of uncertainty in making benefit-cost estimates does not provide sufficient justification for disqualifying them. Surely, rough estimates are better than no estimates.

Another difficulty is that the costs and benefits of environmental regulation are realized at different times. The costs of reducing GHG emissions, for example, are incurred many years before any benefits are derived. Consequently, it is necessary to convert projected costs and benefits to common units (present values) by a process called *discounting*. In principle, the discount rate employed to evaluate a new project should equal the opportunity cost of the investment (*i.e.*, the return available elsewhere). But for public projects, it is difficult to determine precisely the appropriate discount rate. Many analysts choose to use a figure close to the projected real interest rate. Because small differences in the discount rate can produce substantial differences in the present value, it is important that policy alternatives be compared using the same discount rate.

Such concerns about measurement are legitimate, but they fail to address the basic point: It is not sound policy to choose environmental standards without giving consideration to both the costs and the benefits. In a recent *Business Week* editorial, Professor Alan Blinder summed up the situation as follows: "The notion that we must eliminate some environmental hazard 'regardless of the cost' cannot make sense. The only logical approach is to compare costs and benefits and seek out the good deals."[b]

(a) The central estimate for losses in the United States associated with a benchmark doubling of CO_2 seems to be about $18 billion (in 1990 dollars). See William R. Cline, *Global Warming: The Economic Stakes* (Washington, DC: Institute for International Economics, May 1992), p. 33.

(b) Alan S. Blinder, "What Wasn't on the Rio Agenda? A Little Common Sense," *Business Week* (June 29, 1992): 16.

ness investment in order to improve America's economic growth and international competitiveness. **CED believes that regulatory practices such as old- and new-source standards should be reexamined in order to minimize the conflict between environmental regulations and economic growth.**

REGULATORY MECHANISMS FOR CONTROLLING EMISSIONS

Having set goals or standards, regulators must then develop control mechanisms. The traditional approach for controlling emissions is for the regulatory authority to impose a legal limit on the amount of pollutant that an individual source is allowed to emit. In some instances, a particular technology is required.

This traditional command-and-control regulatory approach has several major shortcomings. In recent years, there has been a growing interest in regulatory mechanisms that employ market incentives, reflecting recognition that such regulations are frequently substantially less expensive than command-and-control mechanisms. For example, the 1990 Clean Air Act Amendments address the acid rain problem by creating marketable pollution control permits to reduce SO_2 emissions, primarily from electric utilities. Use of this market mechanism is expected to reduce control costs sharply.[18]

In contrast with command-and-control regulatory methods, economic incentives tend to *automatically* distribute the burden of pollution control in a least-cost manner. Economic incentives also encourage individual sources to develop new technologies to reduce the cost of controlling emissions. **For these and other reasons, CED favors the use of decentralized market mechanisms whenever practicable to reduce emissions, rather than centralized command-and-control regulations.**

COMMAND-AND-CONTROL REGULATION

Command and control can take several forms: (1) regulations that specify the technology to be used by pollution sources to reduce emissions (*e.g.,* setting engineering standards), (2) regulations that specify a performance to be attained based on the performance achievable through use of a particular technology (technology-based performance standards), and (3) regulations that specify the allowable emission levels for each source and leave it to the individual polluter to determine the means for achieving them (performance standards).

The principal advantage of the command-and-control approach is that it is often easy to administer. Regulatory authorities need only set the standard and then follow up on compliance. However, compliance costs for polluters and for society as a whole cannot easily be minimized with such regulations. For command-and-control regulations to achieve a given reduction in *total* emissions at the least cost, regulators would have to set a different requirement for *each source* because *emissions from each source would have to be set at a level that equalizes the marginal cost of reducing emissions from all sources.*[19] If incremental costs of pollution abatement were equalized for all emitters, the largest reductions in emissions would be made by sources that can achieve the goals at the lowest cost, and the smallest reductions would be made by those with the highest costs. But it is virtually impossible for command-and-control mechanisms to achieve this least-cost solution because regulators do not have sufficient expertise and information about the specific costs from each source.

Command-and-control regulation may also discourage the development of lower-cost technology. If regulation uses engineering standards, for example, there may be no incentive for polluters to seek alternative technological options or to redesign production processes to achieve the same (or greater) emission control at a lower cost. Pollution control technology is constantly being improved, so centralized mandating of a specific technology is likely in the longer term to slow down environmental improvement.

Where technology-specific or technology-based mandates are in effect for new or modified installations only, such as the Clean Air Act's New Source Performance Standards (NSPS), there is an incentive for owners of existing sources not to retire old, polluting equipment — a situation that threatens a worsening of air quality rather than an improvement.[20] The problem is further exacerbated if this should lead to even more stringent standards for the new sources. This so-called new-source bias came about because it was acknowledged that the cost of retrofitting existing plants and equipment was unacceptably high. Retrofitting therefore may not be a cost-effective way to correct that bias.

Estimates have been made of the potential cost advantages of decentralized market approaches in various instances where the command-and-control method was used to regulate air pollution. A survey of 11 of these studies found an average cost ratio of command-and-control to least-cost mechanisms (disregarding the two outermost results) of almost 5 to 1.[21]

THE ADVANTAGE OF ECONOMIC INCENTIVES

A number of regulatory techniques provide economic incentives to limit emissions (see "Market Mechanisms for Reducing Pollution," page 42). Each has advantages and disadvantages, and none is a complete answer to the regulatory problems. The two mechanisms recommended most often are *tradable emission permits* and *emission charges*. These mechanisms provide an incentive for business to reduce emissions, but they leave the decision on the means entirely to the firm. If the market value of the permits or the emission charge reflects the social cost of pollution, the social costs will be "internalized" (*i.e.,* included in the price of the product) and economic efficiency improved.

An emission charge encourages each source to reduce emissions up to the point where the cost of further reductions equals the charge. The emission trading mechanism encourages each firm to reduce emissions until the incremental cost of reduction equals the market price of the tradable permits. *Thus, market mechanisms tend to equalize marginal costs across sources of pollution and thereby achieve a given reduction in emissions at the least cost.* Of course, this outcome will be achieved only if firms actually do minimize production costs and if the market for pollution rights functions well. The profit incentive encourages such behavior in most private firms. However, this may not be the case for regulated companies such as electric utilities, which account for a substantial proportion of atmospheric emissions. **CED believes it is essential that public utility regulation be administered in a manner that encourages the utilities to respond to such market incentives to reduce emissions.**

Two frequently used control mechanisms are *product charges* and *subsidies*. These regulatory tools may be politically convenient ways to discourage pollution. But market incentives that apply to products are decidedly less cost-effective than mechanisms that apply directly to emissions (such as emissions trading and emissions charges), and subsidies fail to internalize the social costs of pollution (see "Market Mechanisms for Reducing Pollution.") **CED recommends that regulators use market mechanisms other than product charges and subsidies whenever possible.**

CONSISTENT TREATMENT OF AIR POLLUTANTS AND SOURCES

Although nonutility sources account for about 20 percent of sulphur oxide emissions (see Figure 23, page 25), they are not subject to either the mandatory emissions controls or tradable allowance provisions that apply to utilities under Title IV of the 1990 Amendments. Choosing a regulatory target on the basis of convenience or visibility can be very costly. For example, it has been estimated that under Clean Air Act provisions which came into effect in 1981, mandated reductions of carbon monoxide and nitrogen oxide emissions from motor vehicles cost $2.4 billion annually *more* than if the emissions control had been allocated entirely to stationary sources.[22] In principle, the equalization of marginal costs across sources of a particular pollutant is the least-cost solution for allocating abatement responsibility only if *all* major sources are taken into account.

A least-cost strategy should take into account the fact that many air pollution problems are caused by multiple pollutants. For example, both sulphur dioxide and nitrogen oxides contribute to acid rain. The costs and benefits of an emissions reduction strategy to ameliorate acid rain will not be optimized if sulphur dioxide and nitrogen oxides are treated differently. But this is what happens under Title IV because emissions trading applicable to sulphur dioxide is not permitted for nitrogen oxides.[23] *

DISPOSITION OF REVENUES

Although there is widespread agreement that emissions charges are an efficient mechanism for correcting excessive emissions of pollutants, the question of how to use the resulting revenues is politically very contentious. Should revenues be placed in the general fund or earmarked for more special purposes, such as environmental protection? Some argue for a neutral outcome, whereby revenues derived from emission charges would be offset by cuts in existing, more distorting taxes.[a] There is a fear that if pollution charges are viewed as a revenue device, tax authorities might attempt to increase charges far above levels needed to compensate for the social costs of pollution and thereby defeat the purpose of the charge. Tradable emission permits would also be a source of public revenue if the permits were issued through public auction, as some suggest. The 1990 Clean Air Act distributed permits for SO_2 emissions without charge to existing sources, thereby avoiding the necessity for *government* to resolve the revenue issue.

(a) For further discussion, see Wallace E. Oates, *Pollution Charges as a Source of Public Revenue*, Discussion Paper QE92-05 (Washington, DC: Resources for the Future, 1991).

---

* See memorandum by ROCCO C. SICILIANO (page 94).

In summary, **CED believes that as far as possible, the marginal costs of control should be equalized across sources and across all pollutants that contribute to a specific environmental problem.**

ADDRESSING DISTRIBUTIONAL IMPACTS OF REGULATION

The costs of environmental regulation are not equally distributed among affected firms and consumers, and the benefits do not necessarily accrue to those who pay the costs. This means that the design of environmental policies is affected by the competing interests of potential gainers and losers, leading to higher overall societal costs. A prominent example is the 1977 Amendment to the Clean Air Act that effectively required new coal-fired utilities to install scrubbers in order to meet the NSPS. The lower-cost alternative for satisfying the

---

MARKET MECHANISMS FOR REDUCING POLLUTION

Emissions Trading. The regulatory authority sets a cap on the total emissions level for a particular geographic area and divides the total among existing sources, either by auction or free of charge. It then allows a market to develop for pollution rights. The philosophy behind emissions trading is that a given level of environmental protection can be achieved at less cost if pollution sources with relatively high control costs are able to purchase reductions from sources with relatively low control costs. Expansion of production capacity that created a new emissions source would still be allowable so long as the additional emissions were *offset* by a reduction (*i.e.*, using emission reduction credits elsewhere in the same area). Apart from this policy of *offsets* for nonattainment areas, there are three other principal underpinnings to the U.S. emissions trading system: *bubbles*, within which trading is allowed between *existing* sources; *netting*, whereby burdensome requirements for modification of an existing source can be avoided by reducing emissions at another point or points within the same plant; and *banking*, which allows firms to save emission reduction credits for future use.

In the United States, the idea for emissions trading originally developed as a way to enable new plants to establish themselves in nonattainment areas. The Clean Air Act of 1990 also introduces this mechanism to control SO_2 emissions in order to reduce acid deposition. Although these pollution permits are issued free of charge, they have a market value; therefore, their use raises (opportunity) production costs. Thus, the costs of pollution are internalized with this mechanism.

In spite of the complexity of the administration and operation of emissions trading, evidence of cost savings is widely reported in areas with experience with this mechanism.[a] The program seems to have been effective in its goal of enabling firms to set up in nonattainment areas, since about 2,500 offset trades have been reported.[b]

Emission Charges. These charges are based on actual quantities of pollutant emitted into the atmosphere. Profit-maximizing firms will cut pollution until the incremental cost just equals the tax. Thus, the burden of reducing pollution is distributed in a least-cost manner. If the tax equals the societal cost of pollution, these costs are also fully internalized. Like emissions trading, such a charge is neutral among means for reducing emissions and should therefore encourage use of the most efficient methods.

Ideally, the regulatory authority would have prior information on the amount of emissions that would result from a given tax level in order to set a tax that elicits a specific environmental outcome. Without such information, tax rates may have to be set and reset by trial and error, with repercussions for the planning horizons and productivity of affected businesses.

The difficulties inherent in implementing a system of emission charges have limited the number of practical applications in the area of air pollution. It has been suggested that emission charges be used as adjuncts to other regulations in helping to curb pollution in nonattainment areas. The revenues raised could be used for research and development or recycled as subsidies to help firms install pollution control technology. Such a system has been tried in France, but the tax was too low to yield a positive environmental outcome.[c] As a practical matter, emission taxes, like some command-and-control regulations, are easier to administer when applied to large

---

NSPS — switching from high-sulphur to low-sulphur coal — would have endangered the jobs of miners of high-sulphur coal in the Midwest and Appalachia. One estimate suggested that the cost to the taxpayer of fully compensating the affected miners for their lost annual income would have amounted to less than one-tenth of the cost of installing the scrubbers.[24] The miners were again protected in the acid rain provisions of the 1990 Amendments.

Midwest plants received an additional 200,000 annual SO_2 allowances for five years.

CED believes that regulations should not prohibit business from choosing least-cost options. If such regulatory reform has adverse distributional effects, this problem should be addressed through economic adjustment policies, such as training for those affected, rather than through distortion of energy or environmental policies.

---

stationary sources than to sources that are small and diffuse.

A carbon tax, which has frequently been proposed as the most efficient mechanism for reducing CO_2 emissions, is very similar to an emissions charge. To minimize administrative costs, the tax would be levied on the carbon content of fossil fuels at the point of production (or importation), rather than at the point of consumption.

Product Charges. These are taxes on products (or product characteristics) that are polluting while being produced or consumed. Examples are the tax on cars with low fuel economy and fuel taxes.[(d)] Although taxes based on characteristics of vehicles (*e.g.*, weight) may be convenient, they are not efficient mechanisms for reducing pollution because they are not linked directly to emissions that cause environmental damage. **CED believes that taxes on emissions are preferable to taxes on vehicles.** Taxes on emissions also do not discriminate against any particular use or type of energy, and they encourage the development of cleaner fuels.

Like emission taxes, fuel taxes do not correctly internalize costs of pollution unless they are based on an accurate estimate of those costs. Using fuel taxes to reach a particular level of ambient air quality is also very difficult because consumer responses to different price levels cannot be anticipated in advance with precision, particularly as those responses will be influenced by the availability of more cost-effective technology. Fuel taxes do have the obvious administrative advantage over emission taxes in that they are more easily applied to numerous, small, and diffuse sources, such as motor vehicles. At the same time, they may be regressive in their disproportionate impact on particular groups. (For a detailed discussion of gasoline taxes, see Chapter 4.)

Subsidies. Financial assistance to polluters, in the form of grants, low-interest loans, or tax breaks, is designed either to alter behavior or to help finance compliance with direct regulation. (In the latter case, they do not qualify as economic-based incentives.) Subsidies are widely applied in OECD countries other than the United States as an environmental policy instrument. However, subsidies that finance private-sector pollution control investments out of general government revenues do not internalize the costs of pollution, and sources have no incentive to take these costs into account in their production and consumption decisions. In shifting the cost burden from the polluter to the tax system, this type of subsidization runs contrary to sound regulatory principles.

(a) However, the U.S. experience with emissions trading has been limited. Emissions trading for some pollutants has been allowed since the early 1980s, but so far the number of trades has been relatively small. There are several reasons for this; one is the condition that new sources can only use emission reduction credits to compensate for residual emissions *after* satisfying conventional NSPS requirements.

For a survey of savings estimates from the emissions trading program, see OECD, *Economic Instruments for Environmental Protection* (Paris, France: OECD, 1989), p. 92. See also Hahn and Noll, *Environmental Markets in the Year 2000*, pp. 6-8.

A lead trading program for oil refiners also operated with some success from 1982 to 1987 as a mechanism for reducing the lead content of gasoline.

(b) As many as 12,000 instances of netting have also been reported. See R. Hahn and G. Hester, "Marketable Permits: Lessons for Theory and Practice," *Ecology Law Quarterly* 16, no. 2 (1989): 361-406.

(c) OECD, *Economic Instruments for Environmental Protection*, pp. 35-36.

(d) Fuel taxes have been instituted throughout the OECD for energy conservation and revenue generation, as well as to achieve environmental objectives.

VISIBILITY OF THE COSTS OF ENVIRONMENTAL REGULATION

In order for the public to make informed judgments about environmental controls, they should be aware of the full costs and benefits before the regulation is enacted. In the case of existing regulations, regulatory authorities should make every effort to make the full costs and benefits of regulations visible. In many cases, however, this is not done. For example, purchasers of new motor vehicles are not likely to know how much CAFE adds to the price. **This is another reason CED favors market mechanisms: Command-and-control regulations frequently conceal compliance costs, whereas taxes and charges expose them.**

EFFICIENCY IN ENERGY USE

Pollution abatement can be achieved by either *preventive* or *curative* measures. Preventive options reduce emissions either by lowering the quantity of primary energy required to produce a unit of output or by substituting less polluting fuels. Curative options, such as scrubbers for power plants and catalytic converters for autos, reduce emissions by treating and removing pollutants before they are released into the environment. Such add-on technologies are normally associated with a loss of energy efficiency; for example, three-way catalytic converters increase vehicle fuel consumption by about 5 to 10 percent. Flue gas desulphurization (scrubbing) is estimated to consume 0.75 to 2.7 percent of gross power output.[25]

Enhanced energy efficiency within a plant may be achieved by the application of technology or simply through better energy management. In either case, the energy savings represent a reduction in the cost of pollution abatement. Environmental regulations will encourage this by giving plants credit for reducing emissions by saving energy. Performance standards that set a limit on emissions of a pollutant per unit of flue gas or per unit of energy input will not normally encourage energy-efficiency measures. Technology mandates such as scrubbers will also offer no efficiency incentives.*

Where possible, regulatory standards and instruments should be designed to encourage the selection of the lowest-cost abatement options, which often include emissions reductions achieved by improving energy efficiency, rather than by installing "end-of-pipe" control equipment. Timing of implementation is important. If regulations require that measures be taken too quickly, polluters are less likely to be able to develop innovative solutions and may instead fall back on preexisting curative technologies, thus driving up the cost of pollution abatement.

ENVIRONMENTAL POLICY AND THE FEDERAL STRUCTURE

In the United States, local governments became involved in pollution matters long before the federal government entered the picture. Today, we have a patchwork of federal and local responsibility.[26] In some cases, responsibility is shared by federal and local governments. The National Ambient Air Quality Standards, for example, are established by the EPA but are monitored and enforced largely by state governments. Although there are sometimes gains to be realized from adoption of local standards (see pages 37-38), intervention by state and local governments does not always serve the interests of efficiency or equity. For example, a local government entity may have jurisdiction over a polluting factory but not over all the persons harmed by that pollution. It will consequently not be able to accurately assess either the costs and benefits of regulation or their distribution. At the same time, regulation at the federal level may also be inappropriate. In the example of the polluting

---

* See memorandum by LEON C. HOLT, JR. (page 95).

44

factory, the federal government has jurisdiction over the source of the pollution and all the affected persons but is probably too distant and uninformed about local conditions to mandate the most cost-effective abatement solution.

Clearly, then, some guidelines are needed to ensure that government intervention occurs at the level best able to administer a solution that is both efficient and takes into account all persons incurring damage from the pollution. **CED supports the principle that regulation of a particular air pollution problem should occur at the lowest level of government with jurisdiction over all sources of the pollution and all potential beneficiaries of controlling it. In some cases, this applies to both standards and mechanisms. But in other instances, effective standards are set at the higher level, and implementation is carried out at lower levels of government.**

Local and state governments should be able to use their knowledge of specific local conditions and their proximity to the affected firms and individuals to craft the most efficient and equitable solutions to local problems. Environmental problems that cover a broader geographic area would be left to higher levels of government. At the end of this continuum would be global issues, such as climate change and ozone depletion, which require coordinated action by the entire international community.

It should be acknowledged that many of the recent initiatives at the state and local levels are responses to what is perceived by some as inactivity at the federal level. There is also a certain amount of political gaming whereby some participants hope to force the national government to adopt change by affecting regional policy; technical standards adopted in a critical state, such as California, may preclude a different approach at the national level or in other regions. The result may be to raise compliance costs far above regional benefits.

PRIORITIES FOR ENVIRONMENTAL PROTECTION

There is great political pressure to solve all environmental problems simultaneously, though the available resources are limited. Trying to do everything at once spreads resources too thin; and consequently, major problems sometimes are not addressed satisfactorily. Priorities need to be set. **CED believes that scarce societal resources invested in a cleaner environment should be channeled into those programs that will yield the highest net benefits to society**.

CONCLUSION

The reforms needed to achieve the most cost-effective environmental regulations have been understood for many years. Individuals may differ in their appreciation of the benefits of a quality environment; but given the scarcity of resources, we all should oppose any waste of resources in environmental regulation. Thus, the fact that reform has been painfully slow in coming is surprising. In fact, some critics of present regulatory mechanisms have become so discouraged by "this political preference for inefficiency as driven by a desire to conceal the true costs of regulation" that they question the motivation of the players in the political process.[27] Our view is not that political players have destructive intentions, but that we have failed to keep our eye on the basic objective of environmental regulation. Environmental regulation is not an appropriate instrument for achieving other goals, such as income distribution, industrial development, or a trade advantage, no matter what the individual merits of such goals. Other policies can address such issues. It is time to get on with the objective of achieving a quality environment with the most cost-effective regulation.

POLICIES TO ADDRESS FIVE CRITICAL ISSUES

Government policies on energy and the environment rarely conform with the principles of sound regulation described in Chapter 3. Regulations that have profound effects on our society have often been put in place with little or no attempt to subject them to systematic analysis of benefits and costs or to employ the most cost-effective methods of control. Instead, the choice of regulatory standards generally reflects a political compromise, sometimes constrained by technical feasibility, with emphasis on convenience rather than scientific evidence and economic principles. Stationary and mobile sources of local pollution are covered by separate regulations that treat the same type of emission differently, and some important sources of emissions are simply not controlled. Market incentives, which permit greater flexibility and lower costs, have been employed as a control mechanism in only a few instances.

The nation is now embarking on a costly program to achieve further reductions in local air pollution. It is also debating alternative policies to address climate change, an issue complicated by exceptional scientific uncertainty. In view of the high costs entailed, it is no longer acceptable to propound environmental regulations that are not cost-effective. Fortunately, the political atmosphere may be changing. The public and its political representatives now appear to be more cognizant of the need to consider trade-offs among policy alternatives. Some in the environmental community seem to be moving toward greater appreciation of market incentives as a regulatory mechanism, and the business community seems to be more determined to achieve a clean environment. We believe that the barriers to sound policy can be overcome through improved public understanding of the potential saving to society.

Over the years, environmental regulations have been enacted in a piecemeal fashion in response to current problems; consequently, there is no unifying economic philosophy underlying these regulations. In this chapter, we examine government policies and recommend regulatory reforms in five areas: global climate change, energy efficiency and the atmosphere, motor vehicle emissions and fuel efficiency, nuclear energy, and renewable energy. This is by no means an exhaustive list of policy areas. However, individually or taken together, they are of sufficient importance that the choice of policies will have a significant impact on the cost of energy-related control measures.

GLOBAL CLIMATE CHANGE

The prospect of global climate change brought about by human activity is one of the most challenging issues facing policy makers. The IPCC's projection indicates that GHG concentrations could be twice as high as preindustrial levels as early as 2025. The IPCC and National Academy of Sciences reports indicate that with a considerable time lag, such an increase in GHG concentrations could have significant effects on the earth's climate, including a rise in average global temperatures, perhaps by the middle of the next century. But scientists are quite divided about the magnitude of the effects on climate. Some scientists believe that the IPCC projections of climate change are too pessimistic. Unfortunately, the combination of this scientific uncertainty and the politically charged atmosphere of environmental policy raises the probability of costly policy errors, either because of unwarranted neglect of the problem or because of inappropriate regulations to an uncomfortably high level. However, CED believes that the principles of sound regulation provide a basis for a rational policy response that limits the potential for policy errors.

The issue of global climate change cannot be addressed successfully without the cooperation of many nations. Not surprisingly, there is considerable disagreement in the international community on both objectives and policy mechanisms. The European Community, Japan, and many other nations advocate specific national targets for reductions in GHG emissions. But the targets differ, and some question whether all these nations have made a serious commitment. Others, including the U.S. government at the time of the UNCED conference in Rio, believe that there is too much scientific uncertainty and that the potential cost is too high to warrant the adoption of emission targets at the present time. Some developing countries look upon global climate change as an opportunity to shift technology and wealth from rich nations to poor nations, which are often very inefficient users of energy.

As demonstrated by negotiations for the framework convention on climate change, the diversity of national circumstances and goals makes it difficult to achieve international agreement on GHG emissions. GHG emissions result from a broad range of basic economic activities, the curtailment of which would have a significant impact on the economic interests of every country. For many nations, especially developing countries, the economic cost of reducing GHG emissions would be a considerable burden, and the benefits are not certain. It is unlikely that all nations would benefit equally from a reduction, and some may even believe, perhaps incorrectly, that they would benefit from global warming.

BASIC OPTIONS

The policy options available to address climate change can be divided into five categories:

- Scientific data collection and research, involving improved understanding of factors that affect global climate and the impact of climate change on ecological systems, economies, and societies

- Climate engineering, which would attempt to offset the effect of rising emissions of GHGs on climate by technological means, such as placing particulates in the stratosphere to screen the earth from solar radiation

- Adaptation, which would involve responding to climate change by such actions as moving people from regions that become arid, developing drought-resistant crops, and building dikes to prevent rising ocean levels from destroying coastal property

- Low-cost mitigation measures to reduce GHG emissions, including no regrets policies that should be undertaken for other reasons regardless of climate change; and

- More stringent and costly emission control policies, preferably market-based control measures such as a carbon tax

Scientific Research. The description of the basic science of global climate change contained in the reports of the National Academy and the IPCC (see Chapter 2) seems to be widely accepted by informed scientists. Scientists generally agree that with a considerable time lag, increased concentrations of GHGs will cause some degree of climate change, including a rise in average global temperatures. Unfortunately, the magnitude, regional distribution, and timing of those changes are highly uncertain. The reliability of general circulation models, from which most projections are derived, is an unsettled issue. The IPCC estimates that mean surface-air temperatures have risen 0.3° to 0.6° centigrade during the last century, and its report indicates that temperatures could rise by about 0.3° centigrade per decade in the future if emission trends continue. Some scientists believe that the effect on the climate is likely to be much smaller. The debate appears to be about the magnitude and timing, not the direction, of the change. The George C. Marshall Institute, perhaps the strongest critic of the IPCC projections, presents its argument as follows:

> It is clear that since the greenhouse gases have a heat-insulating effect, some degree of warming is likely to occur if their concentration in the atmosphere is increased. The question is: How much? If the greenhouse effect were as large as the commonly accepted forecasts predict, it would have produced a clear greenhouse signal in the temperature records of the last 100 years. But the signal is not present. Apparently, the greenhouse effect is considerably smaller than has been estimated. [1]

The U.S. government has been the leading sponsor of research on global climate change, providing more than half of the financing worldwide. The United States has spent over $2.6 billion since 1990, and an additional $1.4 billion was proposed for fiscal 1993. Its program is aimed at (1) gathering data to document global climate change, (2) increasing understanding of key global climate processes, (3) improving the ability to forecast global and regional climate and environmental changes, and (4) providing an ongoing assessment of scientific knowledge and implications for policy. **CED strongly supports the U.S. government's interdisciplinary research program and urges it to encourage other industrial countries to increase their research funding as part of any international agreement on climate change.**

It is hoped that during the next decade, the ongoing research effort will greatly improve our understanding of and ability to project global climate change. But scientists' understanding of climate change did not move ahead as rapidly as expected in the last decade. Thus, as with many other environmental problems, policy makers may be forced to take action well before many areas of uncertainty are completely resolved.

Climate Engineering. The National Academy has concluded that climate engineering appears to have considerable potential for off-setting global warming at low cost but that the side effects, especially chemical reactions in the atmosphere and effects on the ecology, are not known. Therefore, the Academy has recommended further research and warned that such options should be considered with great care.[2] **CED agrees with the recommendation for further research on climate engineering.**

Adaptation. The adaptation option appears to have some merit for highly industrialized countries. Advanced economies currently prosper in a wide range of climatic conditions, and they have the resources to adjust to gradual climate change within the range projected by the IPCC. However, the National Academy concluded that although advanced industrial countries may be able to adapt to the climate change projected by the IPCC "without great economic hardship," climate change in the upper end of the projected range "may overwhelm human adaptive mechanisms in areas of marginal productivity and countries where traditional coping mechanisms have been disrupted."[3] Even for advanced industrial nations, adaptation policies may not provide sufficient protection against possible severe effects of global warming, which seem to be unlikely but cannot be ruled out. Moreover, a decision to rely on adaptation policies does not lead to the conclusion that all action should be postponed. It may be possible, for example, to reduce future costs of adaptation substantially by altering the present design and construction of coastal highways and bridges. But present spending on adaptation policies may not be as cost-effective as low-cost mitigation policies.

Mitigation Measures. Given the slow response of GHG concentrations in the atmosphere to changes in emission rates, mitigation policies can succeed only if taken many years before any climate change occurs. But because of the unusual degree of scientific uncertainty, the implementation of high-cost mitigation options is inherently risky.

The uncertainty concerning the benefits of reducing GHG emissions has led many to believe that proposals for actions to reduce GHG emissions are premature and nearly certain to lead to inefficient programs. They advise waiting until better scientific evidence of global climate change is available. It would be incorrect, however, to conclude that a high degree of uncertainty about the benefits of lower GHG emissions is a reason for opposing *all* actions to slow emissions, especially low-cost measures, or for believing that efficient mitigation policies are beyond possibility. The nature of the uncertainty itself sheds some light on the advisability of preventive policies.

- Increased GHG emissions are expected to affect climate only after a very long lag, and concentrations cannot be reduced quickly because some GHGs, especially CO_2, persist in the atmosphere for exceedingly long periods. **This information suggests that a delay of a few years before taking action would not have much effect on the buildup of atmospheric concentrations of GHGs in the next few decades. Nevertheless, delay would involve a continuously rising risk because we are not certain how much future warming is already built into the system and because beyond some point, feedback effects could accelerate the temperature rise.**[4]

- Climate change projected by the IPCC and the National Academy could cause substantial hardship in certain highly vulnerable countries. **This circumstance makes it very questionable for advanced industrial countries to oppose no-cost and very low-cost mitigation programs.** Moreover, even highly industrialized countries face some risk. Indeed, the National Academy study concluded that serious consequences, including catastrophic occurrences, cannot be ruled out.[5] **This suggests that it is rational to take some preventive action as insurance against the possibility of serious occurrences.** Such action has been compared to the behavior of a property owner who buys fire insurance even though he believes that the probability of fire is very low. (But the payoff for mitigation of emissions is lower damage, rather than compensation for damage.)

- The major sources of man-made GHGs, particularly CO_2, are well known in most countries. The concentration of these gases in the atmosphere is also known with a relatively high degree of certainty. **This information suggests that efficient methods of reducing emissions could be designed.**

There is also the possibility that postponing all action for an extended period might result in the need for very strict and far more costly controls at a later time. But how much action is justified? Because of uncertainty and limits on available resources, the Bush Administration embraced a no regrets policy.[6] In 1990, the President's Council of Economic Advisers stated that a program which limits the growth of GHG emissions and at the same time "yields non-greenhouse benefits commensurate with its costs" is the best short-run way to address the potential problem of global climate change.[7] Critics of this approach say that such a policy does not recognize any added benefit from reducing greenhouse gases. However, this policy could have a significant impact on GHG emissions if the programs that yield non-greenhouse benefits are given a higher priority because of their effect on the emissions of GHGs.

CED believes that existing scientific uncertainty is not a reason for postponing all action to mitigate GHG emissions. Low-cost action should be taken promptly in order to reduce the potential impact of climate change on the most vulnerable countries. We also believe further study should be undertaken on more radical control mechanisms that may be needed in the future as insurance against possible severe and irreversible damage. Given the potential cost of delay, work on the design of such measures should not be postponed.

EFFICIENT MECHANISMS FOR CONTROLLING GHG EMISSIONS

The principles of regulation endorsed by CED argue strongly for market-based emission control mechanisms, such as emission charges or tradable emission permits. However, there are opportunities for reducing GHG emissions at an even lower cost. **These low-cost options should be given first priority in any program to reduce GHG emissions.**

Low-Cost Options. There is widespread agreement that the initial reductions in global emissions of CO_2 could be achieved at very little or even no cost. Clearly, the most cost-effective control measures should be taken before moving to more costly mechanisms. The most frequently mentioned low-cost measures for reducing GHG emissions are: (1) the removal of price supports and government subsidies for fuels with a high carbon content, (2) government policies to encourage cost-effective improvements in the efficiency of energy use and in renewable energy, (3) the liberalization of trade in order to increase the availability of technology to improve pollution control, energy efficiency and non-polluting energy sources, (4) an international accord to reduce deforestation, and (5) a program to reduce population growth worldwide.

In Eastern Europe and in many developing countries, fossil fuels are frequently sold far below global market prices. Such subsidies encourage inefficient use of energy and excessive CO_2 emissions. Several developing countries are also reported to subsidize deforestation activity, an important source of CO_2 emissions. The World Bank estimates that all energy subsidies cost developing countries, including the former Soviet Union and Eastern Europe, "more than $230 billion per year — more than four times the total world volume of official development assistance." The former USSR and Eastern Europe account for the bulk of these subsidies, about $180 billion.[8]

Even advanced industrial countries provide subsidies that encourage CO_2 emissions. According to International Energy Agency calculations, Germany, Japan, Spain, and the United Kingdom spent $11.2 billion on coal industry subsidies in 1991. In the cases of Germany and Japan, this translates to about $105 per metric ton of coal produced in those countries.[9] Removal of such subsidies would be justified on economic efficiency grounds even if there were no environmental benefits. Thus, for a nation (though not for individual workers in the industry), the elimination of these subsidies is a win-win policy.

The potential for lowering CO_2 emissions by reducing subsidies appears to be very large. The World Bank estimates that more than half of the air pollution in developing countries is attributable to energy subsidies and other distortions and that removal of all subsidies, including those on coal in industrial countries, would cut worldwide carbon emissions from energy use by 10 percent.[10] **CED strongly recommends that the U.S. government urge all nations to eliminate fuel subsidies that encourage emissions of GHGs, primarily because of the beneficial environmental effects but also because of the added benefit of improving economic efficiency.**

Despite the existing market incentives for business and consumers to adopt cost-effective energy-efficiency measures, there still appear to be significant untapped opportunities for improvement. Government can play a role in encouraging efficient energy use by providing technical information and by its own example (see Policy Recommendations, pages 60 to 64). **CED believes that cost-effective improvements in energy efficiency in order to reduce emissions of CO_2 should be strongly encouraged.**

The liberalization of trade and economic reform should also help reduce GHG emissions in the former Communist countries and in developing countries because it will speed the inflow of more energy-efficient equipment and less polluting technology. **CED continues to support U.S. government efforts to liberalize international trade in technology.**

There are a number of other options for reducing CO_2 emissions that are low in cost (measured in dollars per ton of carbon) relative to more radical options. One approach is to protect and expand natural carbon sinks.

There is wide agreement, for example, that one of the lowest-cost methods for reducing GHG emissions is to *reduce deforestation*. In some areas the cost may be as low as $2.30 per ton of carbon emissions reduced. It has been estimated that 700 million tons of carbon emissions could be eliminated annually at a cost of only $6 per ton by ending deforestation in just three countries.[11] This figure is far below estimates of the cost of reducing GHG emissions by controlling emissions from the burning of fossil fuels. **CED believes that the U.S. government should continue to push for a global forest convention in order to lay the groundwork for protecting these critical sinks.** In some regions of the world, *afforestation* projects may also be a relatively low-cost option, particularly if they are justified on other economic grounds.[12] Although the potential effects of individual low-cost measures, such as afforestation, are not particularly large, the combined effects of these programs could be very important.

Carbon Taxes and Tradable Permits. Because some observers believe that low-cost mitigation measures are unlikely to achieve a sufficient reduction in GHG emissions, they recommend the adoption of stricter controls. If scientific research shows that additional controls are needed, the principles of sound regulation strongly support the use of market mechanisms such as emission taxes or tradable permits because of their low cost and flexibility. As explained in Chapter 3, **an effective and efficient regulatory market mechanism would target the emissions rather than the energy source, and it would equalize the marginal cost of reducing emissions across all sources of GHGs. A carbon tax, which is an excise tax on raw fossil fuels based on their relative carbon content, comes very close to meeting the requirements of an efficient control mechanism.** Although it is not a true emission tax, it is proportional to CO_2 emissions when the fuel is burned if no method of reducing emissions is employed. Thus, it would internalize the social costs of CO_2 emissions at the lowest possible cost of compliance. Carbon taxes would appear to consumers as price increases on all fossil fuels, with the amount of the increase depending on carbon content. Although it would not have an impact on other GHGs, a carbon tax would affect a high portion of overall GHG emissions because CO_2 now accounts for more than half of the man-made greenhouse effect and its share is expected to rise sharply.

Unlike command-and-control regulations, a carbon tax would provide the correct market incentives: (1) It would raise the price of carbon-based fuels and thereby encourage economic efficiency in their use. (2) It would fall more heavily on fuels with a high carbon content and, therefore, would encourage consumers to shift from higher- to lower-carbon-content fuels (from coal to oil, from oil to natural gas, from fossil fuels to nonfossil energy sources). (3) It would provide an incentive to develop and introduce new technologies, either to reduce the CO_2 emissions from fossil fuels or to develop alternative energy sources.

Because a carbon tax would probably be imposed at the production (or import) stage, it would initially fall on relatively few economic agents; consequently, it would be relatively easy to administer.[13] Tax revenues would also make the cost of control visible to policy makers and the public, an important improvement over the hidden costs often associated with command-and-control regulation. Over time, the effect of a carbon tax would be to reduce CO_2 emissions, probably at a small fraction of the cost of inefficient command-and-control regulations.

A carbon tax would probably be easier to administer than the alternative market mechanism, tradable permits for CO_2 emissions. Tradable permits would provide more certainty about emission levels but less certainty about compliance costs. Tradable permits would require the development of a new market for permits and new regulatory authority. They would also raise more serious distributional problems because it would be difficult to achieve a mutually agreeable allocation of permits.

A carbon tax appears to be a more flexible control mechanism than tradable permits. For example, if new scientific information suggested the need for tighter controls, it would probably be easier to raise emission charges than to reduce the number (or value) of outstanding tradable permits. Monitoring of emissions under a permit mechanism would also be relatively difficult.[14]

Although a carbon tax appears to meet most of the theoretical requirements for an efficient CO_2 control mechanism, many unresolved issues remain. To begin with, the precise tax rate necessary to achieve a given emission target is not known; the rate could be quite high if the target is tight. The Congressional Budget Office (CBO) simulated a phased-in carbon tax (beginning at $10 per ton in 1991 and rising to $100 per ton in 2000) using several models. The results show that CO_2 emissions would be reduced by an amount ranging from 8 percent below the baseline level to 36 percent below the baseline.[15] It may take many years to develop sufficient information on demand and supply elasticities to be able to identify the required tax. This may not be a critical shortcoming, however, if the initial tax rate is low and changes in rates are phased in slowly. There would be adequate opportunity to make gradual adjustments in rates to reflect new information about appropriate targets and the response of emissions to taxes. Indeed, given the degree of scientific and economic uncertainty about global warming, such flexibility in the control instrument is desirable.

A second problem is the need for international cooperation. A carbon tax would not be effective unless it is adopted by many nations, because actions taken by a single nation or even a group of nations could easily be offset by others if there is no international agreement. A single worldwide carbon tax administered by an international agency is impracticable because most nations would be unwilling to give up sovereignty and control over revenues. Moreover, developing countries that have less information about CO_2 sources and less flexibility may encounter difficulties enforcing a carbon tax. Other effective emission control mechanisms, such as reductions in deforestation, may be more practical for many nations.

The implementation of a carbon tax would be a complex task. Many obstacles would be encountered in international negotiations on a fair and effective carbon tax:

- In many countries, certain fossil fuels are already heavily taxed; consideration would need to be given to existing variations in these implicit carbon taxes.

- There is the free-rider problem, whereby nations that do not reduce emissions would benefit from the actions of those that do. The higher the proposed carbon tax, the greater the incentive for some nations not to participate.

- Nations that did not impose a carbon tax would enjoy a competitive advantage in international trade. Thus, some compensating measures may be necessary.

- Some developing countries may feel it necessary to give priority to economic growth over environmental issues and would not be willing to impose even low-cost reductions in CO_2 emissions unless advanced industrial nations were willing to pay for the program.[16]

Initially, an emission reduction program might be effective if only large industrial nations, which now account for most CO_2 emissions, participate. Given the rapid growth in their use of energy, however, the participation of developing countries will also become critical. In all likelihood, an international agreement would require that a portion of the carbon tax revenues collected by advanced industrial countries be transferred to poor nations in order to ensure that low-cost measures, such as reduced deforestation, are undertaken. However, negotiations for such transfers may be difficult in view of the adverse historical experiences with such transfers and loans to developing countries. There would also be issues concerning what sanctions should be taken against those who fail to cooperate with international restrictions on GHG emissions.

Another major problem is the fact that the world population is projected to grow very rapidly in developing countries and to generate sharp increases in CO_2 emissions that could substantially offset the effects of CO_2 reductions obtained from a carbon tax or other measures. **Thus, consideration should be given to programs to reduce population growth worldwide.**

Finally, there is a great deal of uncertainty about the economic effects of a carbon tax. The tax base is so large that even a small tax could generate considerable revenues. For example, a tax of $10 per ton of carbon would generate about $13 billion at 1991 levels of U.S. emissions. As a consequence, it could have a significant effect on the aggregate economy. Thus, it may be necessary to phase the tax in fairly slowly in order to avoid short-run destabilizing effects. The long-term economic consequences of a carbon tax would depend critically on how the revenues are used. If a carbon tax internalizes the social costs of emissions, it could improve resource allocation. Indeed, many economists believe that the efficiency properties of the overall U.S. tax system could be improved by substituting a carbon tax for taxes that are more distorting.[17]

Because there is considerable variation in the carbon content of fossil fuels (see Table 7), a carbon tax would also place a relatively high burden on workers in industries that produce fuels with a high carbon content. For example, a $30-per-ton carbon tax, which the Congressional Budget Office estimates would generate a cumulative $189.4 billion in revenue by 1998 and stabilize emissions of CO_2 at close to current levels, corresponds approximately to a $19.60 tax per ton of coal, $0.50 per thousand cubic feet (MCF) of natural gas, $3.89 per barrel of oil, and $0.08 per gallon of gasoline. The burden of such a tax would be about 10 percent of the prices of refined petroleum and natural gas and 55 percent of the delivered price of coal.[18] Thus, a carbon tax would cause a shift away from coal and would have a relatively large adverse effect on production and employment in the coal industry. **CED believes that distributional issues should be addressed through economic adjustment policies rather than through the distortion of efficient environmental policies.**

Conclusion. CED urges the U.S. government to study and design a comprehensive contingency plan for reducing GHG emissions.* Top priority should be given to research to reduce scientific uncertainty

Table 7

Carbon Content of Selected Fossil Fuels
Pounds of carbon

	By Volume	By Btu Content [a]	$30 Per Ton Carbon Tax Equals [b]
Coal	1,307.00 (per ton)	5.5	$19.60 (per ton)
Crude Oil	6.18 (per gallon)	4.3	$3.89 (per barrel)
Natural Gas	33.00 (per MCF)	3.2	$0.50 (per MCF)
Gasoline	5.10 (per gallon)	4.0	$0.08 (per gallon)

(a) 10^{-5} pounds per Btu.

(b) The CBO estimates that a tax of $30 per ton, put in place in 1994, would generate more than $40 billion annually by the third year of its implementation.

SOURCE: Adapted from Roger C. Dower and Mary Beth Zimmerman, *The Right Climate for Carbon Taxes: Creating Economic Incentives to Protect the Atmosphere* (Washington, DC: World Resources Institute, August 1992), p. 5, and Congressional Budget Office, *Reducing the Deficit: Spending and Revenue Options* (Washington, DC: CBO, February 1993), p. 404.

*See memorandum by RICHARD J. KRUIZENGA (page 94).

and to low-cost CO_2 mitigation measures. High-cost measures should be implemented only if scientific evidence confirms that global climate change is a serious threat to society and if low-cost control measures prove to be inadequate. If more stringent controls are needed, CED recommends that regulators turn to market-based control mechanisms. The principles of regulation supported in this report indicate that among alternative control options a carbon tax appears to be the most cost-effective method for achieving large reductions in CO_2 emissions. However, more study is needed concerning the problems of implementing a carbon tax. Problems of achieving international cooperation along with issues of transitional and long-run costs, economic effects, revenue recycling, and enforcement deserve further study. If a carbon tax is adopted, great care must be taken to minimize or offset any unintended consequences and to ensure that the desired environmental goals are met. In the meantime, low-cost programs to prevent global warming should be implemented promptly. In our view, there is no reasonable basis for delaying action on these measures. CED believes that if low-cost options are pursued vigorously around the world, a substantial reduction in CO_2 emissions would be achieved. Whether the reduction is sufficient would depend, among other things, on goals sought by policy makers.

IDENTIFYING EFFICIENT GOALS FOR CO_2 EMISSIONS

The IPCC's projections assume that CO_2 emissions will rise from about 7 billion tons of carbon in 1990 to 12 to 15 billion tons by 2025. Many EC and certain other countries have adopted the target of stabilizing CO_2 emissions at 1990 levels by the year 2000. Some scientists, environmentalists, and economists have proposed even more aggressive targets. However, these targets have rarely been based on rigorous studies of the benefits and costs of emission reductions. One reason is that the measurement problems are quite formidable. The costs of reducing emissions can be esti-

mated with a moderate degree of confidence, but estimates of the benefits are far less reliable. This is due to the high degree of uncertainty about the magnitude, timing, and regional distribution of climate change as well as about the damage climate change could do to social, economic, and ecological systems. Nevertheless, the range of benefit and cost estimates provides useful insights on appropriate emission targets.

BENEFIT-COST ESTIMATES OF MITIGATION POLICIES

Evaluation of the benefits and costs of alternative CO_2 emission targets depends on three factors: (1) estimates of the costs of control, (2) estimates of the damage caused by climate change (reduction in damage is the benefit of control), and (3) the rate of discount by which future benefits and costs are given current value. Some studies assume that significant reductions in CO_2 can be attained at relatively low costs largely by improving energy efficiency. But the potential for improvements in energy efficiency that are also cost-effective is an unsettled matter. It is agreed, however, that abatement costs rise sharply as further reductions in emissions are achieved because more costly control measures are required. It is also agreed that large cuts in CO_2 emissions would be very costly, though the range of estimates is fairly wide. For a 20 percent reduction in CO_2 emissions below 1990 levels, abatement cost estimates frequently range from about $100 to $300 per ton of carbon reduced and an eventual GDP loss of 1 percent or more.[19] These estimates are generally based on models that assume the reduction in emissions is achieved by least-cost methods.[20] If command-and-control methods are used, the cost might be substantially higher. Estimates of the damage from global climate change (*i.e.*, the benefit of reducing emissions) are also tentative because of the scientific uncertainty discussed earlier, because the market value of some effects cannot be measured directly, and because a significant portion of the damage accrues to those living in foreign countries. Estimates of the economic damage to the United States as a result of a doubling of GHG concentrations generally range from 1 to 2 percent of GDP. The largest losses would be in agriculture, electricity, water supply, and costs associated with a rise in sea level.

In their research, William Nordhaus[21] and William Cline[22] attempt to provide comprehensive estimates of both the costs and the benefits of mitigation policies. Their estimates are based on the projections of climate change made by the IPCC. Despite the scientific uncertainty and the difficulty of arriving at estimates, both studies find that the initial reduction in GHG emissions can be achieved at a very low cost, and both conclude that the benefits of small reductions would significantly exceed the costs. But the studies differ on estimates of optimal reductions.

Nordhaus compares the costs of reducing emissions with three estimates of the damage caused by GHGs. With the low-damage estimate, he finds that the optimal reduction is quite small; the high-damage estimate calls for a one-third reduction from current levels. The middle or best estimate of damage indicates that the most efficient outcome would be an 11 percent reduction in CO_2 emissions. The costs would likely exceed the social benefits derived from larger reductions. The Cline study supports a more aggressive policy, indicating that a one-third cut in carbon emissions from current levels by the end of the first decade of the next century would be cost-effective. The principal reason for these different estimates appears to be the choice of discount rate.[23]

Such calculations of the benefit-cost ratio of CO_2 mitigation for the United States may not hold for the entire world. The United States does not have a large area of low-level land threatened with flooding as a consequence of a small rise in sea levels. Moreover, output is generally much less sensitive to climatic conditions in advanced industrial countries than in developing countries. For the United States, for example, it is estimated that only 3 percent of output is highly sensitive to climatic change and that the effect is negligible for 87 percent of U.S. output.[24] But agriculture and outdoor activities are among the largest sources of income in the developing countries.[25]

It is sometimes argued that benefit-cost studies underestimate the value of reducing GHG emissions because the damage to the ecology, which cannot easily be quantified, is given too little weight. Some also believe that ancillary benefits of GHG control, such as reduced local pollution, are not given sufficient weight. On the other hand, it is also possible that these studies exaggerate the benefits of reducing emissions because evidence underlying projections of large changes in temperature, primarily computer models of global atmospheric dynamics (general circulation models), is not conclusive.

Conclusion. Currently available evidence is not sufficient to identify an optimal target for reductions in GHGs, though it does appear that a small reduction in CO_2 emissions would have a net benefit for society if it is achieved by an efficient mechanism. Future experience and research will shed more light on the matter of optimal targets. At this time, **it is more important that cost-effective mechanisms for control be put in place in a timely fashion than it is to identify the final goals for emissions reductions.**

ENERGY EFFICIENCY AND AIR QUALITY

Energy efficiency in the United States, measured by the ratio of energy consumption to national output, has improved significantly in recent decades. The desirability of cost-effective improvements in energy efficiency is an objective about which all can agree because improved efficiency offers the opportunity to benefit the environment while improving the performance of the economy. Environmental damage is often reduced simply by decreasing energy consumption, and the performance of the economy is improved by reducing the resources needed to achieve a given output. However, it is important to distinguish between technically feasible improvements in energy efficiency and cost-effective improvements. Many reports that refer to potential improvements in energy efficiency consider only technical feasibility. But if the most advanced energy-saving technology (from an engineering perspective) requires investments whose costs exceed the energy savings, then from the point of view of the individual producer or consumer, the technology is not cost-effective and there is no net gain from its adoption (there is a loss). An important determinant of cost-effectiveness of energy efficiency investments is the cost of fuel, which can be influenced by public policy. As mentioned in the preceding section, increased energy taxes encourage greater energy efficiency.

From a social perspective, measurement of cost-effectiveness should also include the benefits of reduced pollution. If energy prices do not reflect the full social cost of energy consumption (*i.e.*, if the costs of pollution are not internalized), investments that do not appear to be cost-effective from the viewpoint of the individual or firm may be cost-effective from the viewpoint of society. This is a reason for regulators to make sure that prices reflect the full social cost.

The experience of the last few decades shows that consumers do make wise energy conservation investments in response to rising energy prices. Businesses have also responded to market incentives by improving the efficiency of energy use. For example, today's combined-cycle power plants produce electric power with efficiencies close to 55 percent (Lower Heating Value). Furthermore, when burning natural gas, these very high efficiencies are enhanced by low emissions. [26]

However, it is generally believed that the full potential for cost-effective energy efficiency will not be realized by consumers without encouragement from government. If consumers have insufficient information about opportunities for cost-effective investments in energy efficiency, or if they are faced with other nonmarket disincentives, further government initiatives may be needed. Government can encourage efficient investments by making households and businesses aware of opportunities and by ensuring that consumers have access to the technologies and the supporting infrastructure required to adopt and

maintain them. But government must not ignore consumer preferences about attributes of products other than their energy efficiency characteristics. Policies to encourage consumers to invest in energy efficiency have a cost, against which the potential benefits of the policies should be weighed.

Some observers believe that even informed consumers frequently do not opt for investments in energy efficiency that appear to be in their own economic self-interest. The reasons are not well understood and require further study. **CED believes that the role of government should be twofold: (1) to get energy prices to reflect the full social costs of its use and (2) to target information deficiencies and correct any nonmarket disincentives that impede the adoption of energy-efficient products and services. But it should do this without adding bureaucratic inefficiencies.**

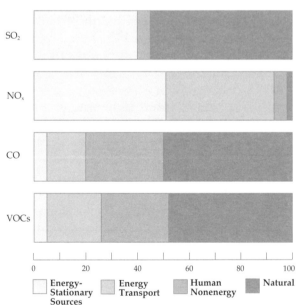

Figure 38

Contributions of Natural and Human Activity to Presence of Selected Pollutants

Percent of total emissions

Estimates for VOCs and NO$_x$ are for the United States. Estimates for SO$_2$ and CO are global.

SOURCE: Environmental Protection Agency and International Energy Agency

The interaction between energy use, emissions, and air quality is very complex. (As Figure 38 shows, natural sources of some pollutants are as important as those arising from human activity.) Consequently, although improved energy efficiency can play a significant role in reducing emissions of common pollutants, the effect on air quality is not easily predicted.[27] CO_2, whose output is directly related to variations in fossil fuel use, and which is not subject to end-of-pipe controls, appears to be an exception.

COMPARING EFFICIENCY ESTIMATES

Estimates of the potential for improving energy efficiency in the United States vary widely. Figures 39 and 40 show alternative projections of U.S. primary energy and electricity consumption over the next 40 years. Electricity is shown separately because it is subject to some of the more spectacular claims regarding energy conservation opportunities. Projections embody different assumptions about the rate at which currently available

efficiency technologies and technologies still in their development phases will be taken up by consumers in the marketplace.

Technical Potential. Some projections of energy consumption are based solely on engineering estimates of long-run savings achievable by replacing all existing stock with the most efficient available technologies. For example, the Energy Information Administration (EIA) characterizes its "very high conservation" case (see Figures 39 and 40) as a demonstration of how much energy saving is technologically feasible but does not claim that this goal can be achieved in the market.[28] The Electric Power Research Institute (EPRI) explicitly states that its projections show what electricity consumption would be if it were somehow possible to replace the entire stock of electric end-use technologies with the most energy-efficient ones by the year 2000.[29] The saving in this case amounts to 24 to 44 percent of EPRI's baseline consumption estimate. The Rocky Mountain Institute's projection of extremely high long-term savings on the

Figure 39

U.S. Energy Consumption, Range of Projections to 2030

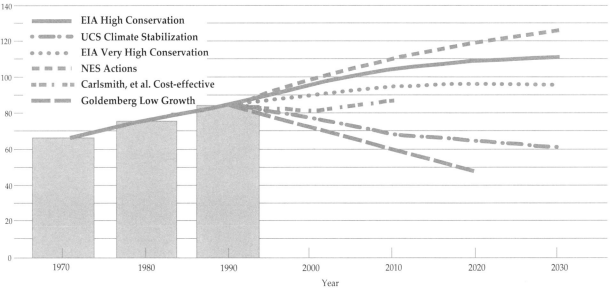

Quadrillion btu

Legend:
— EIA High Conservation
• — • UCS Climate Stabilization
• • • • EIA Very High Conservation
— — — NES Actions
— • — • Carlsmith, et al. Cost-effective
— — — Goldemberg Low Growth

Year

EIA is Energy Information Administration; UCS is Union of Concerned Scientists; NES is National Energy Strategy of the Bush Administration.

order of 75 percent (at very low cost) includes no estimate of the rate of turnover of existing capital stock or of market responses to technology change.[30]

Market Potential. Energy consumption estimates that focus on technical potential only and do not take market conditions and consumer behavior into account are not particularly useful to those responsible for developing regulatory policies. Other projections, shown in Figures 39 and 40, do attempt to estimate the rate at which consumers will actually take up efficiency technologies and reduce consumption. These estimates assume that technologies will be adopted if they are cost-effective, provided that various policies are implemented to help consumers recognize and exploit the opportunities. Cost-effectiveness is usually calculated by comparing the total present value of energy saved with the total cost of the investment.[31] The discount rate employed and energy price projections (both of which are highly uncertain)

are critical to such calculations.

Many believe that the true market potential of energy- efficiency measures is less than suggested by cost-effectiveness estimates because consumers may not implement the measures of their own accord. Consequently, third parties, such as electric utilities, have been encouraged to establish programs to speed the adoption of conservation measures. However, such programs entail a variety of additional costs. For example, some utility-sponsored conservation programs,[32] particularly in the residential sector, have involved unexpectedly high costs to both utilities and consumers. Yet, some of these costs are not included in the accounting of costs by public utilities.[33] Energy savings through application of technologies are also difficult to estimate. Quite apart from the unpredictability of future energy prices, we have inadequate information about consumer utilization patterns and depend on engineering estimates of efficiency performance that are often overoptimistic.[34]

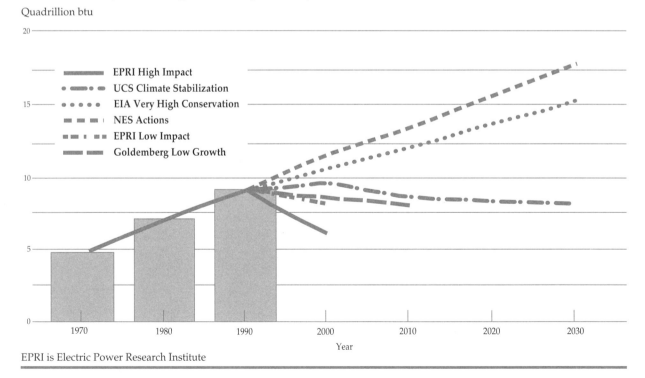

Figure 40

U.S. Electricity Consumption, Range of Projections to 2030

Quadrillion btu

EPRI High Impact
UCS Climate Stabilization
EIA Very High Conservation
NES Actions
EPRI Low Impact
Goldemberg Low Growth

Year

EPRI is Electric Power Research Institute

However, some studies offer a menu of government policy initiatives to move efficiency technologies to the market. It is not certain that we know enough about consumer reactions to be sure that these policies will have the potent impact implied by the more optimistic projections. It is also unclear whether the costs of implementing these policies are fully accounted for in the cost-effectiveness estimates that underlie the projections. Nevertheless, these initiatives may have some positive effects on consumer behavior. There may well be a significant *untapped* potential for improved cost-effective energy conservation in the United States, but the magnitude of that potential depends on how accurately we are able to identify the reasons for consumer reluctance to make energy efficiency investments and how effectively government policies can target them.

EFFICIENCY OPPORTUNITIES AND INVESTMENT DECISIONS

The most frequently cited targets for efficiency are end uses of electricity. Lighting, which accounts for close to one-fifth of all electricity consumption in the United States, is a particularly alluring target. Engineering estimates put the efficiency of certain fluorescent lamps at 50 to 75 percent higher than that of conventional bulbs, with a life span about eight times longer.[35] Yet, residential conservation programs involving lighting and other appliances face significant market barriers and such high costs that they may not be cost-effective.[36]

Electric motors consume up to 70 percent of electricity in the industrial sector. There are reportedly opportunities for substantial savings, particularly by installing motors with adjustable-speed drives that vary power output according to the needs of the specific load. Businesses that are large consumers of energy frequently have found that opportunities for improved energy efficiency exist within their own establishments. The most cost-effective measures are often small projects that tend to be overlooked unless energy efficiency is given high priority or energy prices reach high levels. For example, International Paper Com-

pany recently identified 38 measures that could be implemented at two of its facilities, some of which offered substantial savings at very low cost. Adoption of all the measures would carry an investment cost of just over $5 million, but engineering estimates indicate an *annual* payback of more than $4 million.[37]

Although investments in energy efficiency can generate a high rate of return to the energy consumer, it appears that opportunities for cost-effective investments are still being spurned. From a policy making perspective, an important question is why energy consumers do not take advantage of potential savings. In some cases, this appears to be a rational response to factors such as uncertainty about future energy prices; in other instances, costs may not be estimated correctly. For example, according to some studies, the implied discount rates used to estimate the present value of future energy savings are often too high.[38]

The problem of externalities suggests that if the social cost of using energy is not reflected in the price, consumers will tend to use too much of it and ignore socially efficient opportunities for conservation.[39] In addition to market failures resulting from such externalities, regulated prices may provide inappropriate incentives to consume. Regulators usually apportion a utility's total cost among different classes of customers, setting prices for each at a level that will recover the total cost. This means, in effect, that prices are set at average cost. But if a utility produces its last units of electricity at a marginal cost that exceeds average cost, average-cost pricing encourages overconsumption because the higher marginal costs will not be reflected in the price. Marginal-cost pricing of electricity, together with time-of-use rates, should therefore encourage consumers to increase investments in energy efficiency.[40]

A number of other factors are often cited to explain the failure of consumers to make energy efficiency investments. Some (factors 1 to 3) appear to be the market's reflection of real costs of energy efficiency; others (factors 5 to 7) may be appropriate targets for government action.

1. **Price Risk.** Uncertainty about future energy prices and their effect on the savings from efficiency investments undoubtedly dampens enthusiasm for these investments.

2. **Consumer Preferences.** Factors such as appearance and quality of service tend to be more dominant influences on appliance selection than efficiency characteristics.[41] In the residential and commercial sectors, there may also be divergent incentives for the owner who makes the purchasing decision (and wants to limit capital costs) and the tenant who pays for the energy use over the life cycle of the appliance (and would like to minimize operating costs).

3. **Capital Limitations.** In large industrial firms, energy efficiency projects are just one of a large number of competing investment options to be ranked according to a variety of criteria, some of which are not related to the economic merits of the project (*e.g.*, debt-equity and debt-service ratios).[42] Except in raw materials processing industries, energy usually accounts for less than 5 percent of total production costs. Other, larger capital needs divert management's attention from energy efficiency.

   Residential consumers also face capital constraints. Energy-efficient appliances typically cost more than their less efficient counterparts, and consumers may prefer to incur higher energy costs over the life cycle of the appliance than pay more up front.[43]

4. **Managerial Responsibilities.** In some organizations, there appears to be a problem of getting attention at the decision-making level focused on energy conservation. Energy efficiency ideas are likely to originate at the plant manager level or lower, whereas investment decisions are often made by managers concerned about corporate finance.

5. **Government R&D Spending.** The Department of Energy's budget for conservation R&D fell by 44 percent (not adjusted for inflation) during the 1980s, while R&D expenditures for energy supply declined much less sharply. Spending and tax measures to encourage energy efficiency are a fraction of those for established programs for energy supply.

6. **Supply Infrastructure.** The availability of energy-efficient technologies may be restricted by inertia; for example, there may be a limited number of technicians with the engineering and maintenance skills required to adequately support widespread implementation of the technologies. Also important is the fact that many sellers of energy-efficient goods are small firms without the resources to mass-market their products and services effectively.

7. **Lack of Information.** Companies and residential consumers frequently just do not have sufficient knowledge of the potential for energy savings or the technical solutions for achieving them.

POLICY RECOMMENDATIONS

The oil price shocks of the 1970s prompted an accelerated uptake of energy-efficient technologies and brought about changes in the way consumers used energy. But in the absence of a similar occurrence, improvements in energy efficiency in the United States are likely to proceed only gradually. However, a number of things can be done that are likely to help create greater market opportunities for cost-effective efficiency technologies. The policies that we discuss in this section are exclusively microeconomic, but fiscal policies that keep long-term capital costs down would enable businesses to make a greater number of investments, some of which will be in energy efficiency.[44]

Setting a Government Example. The federal government is by far the largest energy consumer in the United States, spending $8.7 billion a year, including $3.5 billion at its own installations and $4.0 billion in subsidies to low-income households. Although no comprehensive analysis has been made, the Office of Technology Assessment believes that a 25 percent saving could be achieved cost-effectively in federal buildings by using available technologies.[45] State and local governments also use very large amounts of energy. **CED believes that governments at all levels can save energy and money by making cost-effective retrofits at existing facilities and by taking a life-cycle approach to energy investment decisions at new facilities.[46] The emphasis on a cash budget rather than a capital budget in federal decision making may necessitate legislation to ensure that this approach is followed.** It may also be necessary to change government procurement practices so that energy-efficient products will be easier to obtain and to give individuals involved in improving efficiency stronger incentives to do so. These steps would lower the cost of government and make government buildings and houses a de facto showcase for conservation technologies and practices. Moreover, the potentially huge government demand for energy efficiency would contribute greatly to the development of a supply infrastructure and to lowering the cost of efficiency products and services through economies of scale.

Efficiency Standards. The National Appliance Energy Conservation Act of 1987 (NAECA) set minimum efficiency standards (subject to periodic review) for 13 product types, and the 1992 Energy Policy Act mandates standards for others.[47] The failure of consumers to make cost-effective energy efficiency investments often reflects legitimate individual preferences and rational responses to factors such as capital constraints and risk. In setting and updating standards, the federal government should take such factors into account and exercise restraint in overriding these preferences. **CED believes that the role of government in supporting adoption of energy-efficient appliances should be focused on improving the performance of markets and ensuring that consumers have the information needed to make wise purchasing decisions.**

However, in a few instances, appliance standards may recommend themselves. If the full social costs of using electricity are not internalized in the price and electricity is over-consumed as a consequence, efficient appliances would have the effect of reducing consumption in the same way as higher, "correct" electricity prices. In addition, if the incentives for building owners and their tenants in rental markets are at odds, minimum efficiency standards for certain household and commercial appliances that consume very high amounts of electricity would mitigate that problem.

The energy efficiency properties of buildings in the United States are not regulated according to a federal code. Instead, a number of codes have been developed by industry organizations. In many instances, however, failure to update and enforce codes at the state and local levels may considerably diminish efficiency potential.[48] Only about one-third of the states have adopted building codes that meet with standards recommended by the Council of American Building Officials (CABO) and the American Society of Heating, Refrigerating and Air-Conditioning Engineers (ASHRAE), the leading industry organizations.[49] Indeed, many states lack the necessary expertise to keep building codes up to date. In an effort to make up for this deficiency, the Energy Policy Act requires states to update their commercial building codes to bring them into line with the ASHRAE standards. The Department of Energy is to provide technical assistance for this purpose. **The Energy Department's Office of Building Technologies (OBT) should play an active role in providing information and in helping state and local governments to develop up-to-date building codes for both commercial and residential construction. OBT could also assist in training the inspectors who verify compliance with the codes.**

Information Programs. Providing information about efficiency opportunities should continue to be an important part of utility-sponsored conservation programs. The federal government can also play a role. For example, the EPA's Green Lights program, initiated early in 1991, promotes energy-efficient lighting in businesses. Participating companies sign an agreement with the Agency to install lighting upgrades in their facilities wherever it is profitable to do so and within a five-year period. In return, the EPA makes available a range of services, including product information, a registry of financing sources, and technical support. Green Lights gets the appropriate managers involved by making them aware of efficiency opportunities and by giving them publicity when they make such investments. No federal subsidies are involved.[50] **CED supports the creation of such programs for other energy end uses. These programs should work through cooperation with industry organizations that are well positioned to build consensus and to disseminate information about energy-efficient technologies to their members.**

Information programs targeted to residential consumers are not likely to be successful without careful attention to the format and frequency of the information. Media advertising may be less effective than personalized energy audits in the home combined with regular feedback on energy consumption.[51] For these purposes, the remoteness of federal government necessitates the active involvement of state and local authorities, nonprofit organizations, and utilities.

There are significant cost-effective opportunities for energy conservation in electrical appliances such as lighting. Market penetration of efficient appliances faces formidable barriers, including a lack of information and consumer preferences for color and other features that limit the effectiveness of market incentives. Government or utility programs that provide information or other incentives may be desirable. The Federal Trade Commission (FTC) currently has a program mandated by the Energy Policy and Conservation Act of 1975 that provides labels with operating cost ratings for eight different appliances.[52] **CED believes that such labeling programs can be an effective method of informing consumers and making energy efficiency a more important consideration in purchasing decisions.** [53]

Research, Development, and Demonstration. The Department of Energy's conservation research programs have established a good record of developing energy-saving technologies and helping to transfer these technologies to users. Examples include projects involving lighting ballasts, heat pumps, and refrigerators.[54] **CED believes that the federal government should increase R&D support for promising energy efficiency technologies, especially projects at early stages of development that are too risky to be taken on by private companies. We also recommend a federally sponsored market research study to shed more light on consumer responses to energy-efficiency options. This would enable both the government and the electric utilities to target their information and incentive programs effectively and at less cost.**

Energy-Efficient Mortgages. An energy-efficient mortgage is one in which the buyer of a home with superior energy efficiency characteristics qualifies for a larger mortgage, based on the presumption that future energy cost savings will make the higher mortgage payments affordable.[55]

Such mortgage programs have been available in the United States for more than 10 years, but they have been underutilized for a number of reasons: (1) Many lenders and most buyers are not aware of the programs, (2) they involve increased paperwork and are not perceived by lenders to be user-friendly, (3) lenders and buyers are uncertain about energy cost savings, partly because of the lack of a widely agreed upon home energy rating system.[56] The last obstacle is addressed in the 1992 energy bill. **However, the government should use its role in residential mortgage financing to do more to promote conservation investments through energy-efficient mortgages.** The three federal agencies and two secondary mortgage lenders that already have energy-efficient mortgage programs can work together to develop more user-friendly forms and practices.[57] These same institutions can step up their efforts to educate primary lenders, builders, realtors, and home buyers about the availability and benefits of energy-efficient mortgages. They should also collect and analyze data on the financial performance of the existing programs. This would help to determine if there is a higher risk associated with these mortgages and, if necessary, to adjust the loan-to-value formula.

Energy Conservation Programs of Electric Utilities. Cost-effective energy conservation is not only in the customer's self-interest; it can also improve the environment. Many analysts believe that an external stimulus is needed to reduce barriers to investments in cost-effective conservation. Utilities have a prominent role to play in providing information and incentives to encourage consumers to make wise conservation decisions. Marginal-cost pricing, information programs, on-site energy audits, loan financing, direct financial incentives, and other programs designed to mitigate or remove market barriers will help foster energy efficiency improvements and the development of competitive markets.

Utility programs that provide direct financial incentives to customers for the installation of efficient equipment must be cost-effective and promote equitable treatment of all consumers. To ensure such treatment, utility financial incentive programs must not result in an increase in electric rates. This protects nonparticipants as well as those who implemented energy-saving measures before the utility programs were established. Programs that meet this requirement are those whose benefits, in the form of avoided costs, are not only greater than the costs but also make up for revenue losses because of reduced sales (see, for example, "Energy Service Charges"). Avoided costs occur when the costs of generation, transmission, and distribution capacity, as well as energy, are deferred or eliminated as a result of conservation or load-management measures.

In determining the avoided costs associated with utility incentive programs, factors such as free ridership (the extent to which customers receive utility incentives even though they would have installed efficient end-use measures in the absence of the utility programs) and persistence (the extent to which customers take efficiency measures out of service prematurely or do not replace them in kind at the end of their lives) need to be taken into account in order to avoid overestimating the benefits.

For the long term, the promulgation of appropriately high appliance-efficiency standards and building codes, rather than reliance on utility incentive programs, is an equitable

---

ENERGY SERVICE CHARGES

Pacific Power/Utah Power in Portland, Oregon, is pioneering an alternative approach to traditional utility conservation programs. The company's experience with conventional programs that resulted in upward pressure on electricity prices for all consumers — participants and nonparticipants alike — induced it to try a new approach. This is the Energy Service charge. The first step is to have a private energy service contractor carry out a location analysis to identify all cost-effective energy conservation measures. Pacific Power then makes payments to the consumer for installation of the measures and recovers the cost over time by adding an Energy Service charge to the consumer's bill. The charge is set at a level below the value of projected energy savings, resulting in positive cash flow for the consumer.[a] Although cash savings to the individual consumer can be modest in many instances, the total energy savings resulting from a large number of participating consumers are potentially very significant. From the utility viewpoint, the Energy Service charge can be structured to recover the full cost of the efficiency measures plus revenues lost because of reduced consumption. Nonparticipants also benefit because their electricity prices are not affected by conservation program costs or by the costs of additional power.

(a) Note that as part of the agreement between utility and customer, energy savings are monitored in the initial period after installation of the energy efficiency measures to ensure that savings are as anticipated. If not, the service charge is adjusted.

SOURCE: Pacific Power/Utah Power

and effective approach to continuing and institutionalizing energy conservation actions that may not be achieved naturally in the marketplace. **CED recommends that regulators adopt incentive guidelines for conservation programs encouraging utilities to promote programs that do not cause the unit cost of electricity to increase.***

MOTOR VEHICLE EMISSIONS AND FUEL EFFICIENCY

In the United States, public recognition of the energy-environment nexus is perhaps greatest in the transportation field because ownership and use of motor vehicles is very widespread. During the last 30 years, innumerable regulations have been put in place by both state and federal governments for the purpose of reducing motor vehicle emissions and improving vehicle fuel efficiency.[58] Unfortunately, regulators have emphasized inefficient command-and-control measures to achieve a variety of goals. At one point, the objective was to reduce urban pollution; this resulted in emission standards and technical control mechanisms on new vehicles. Later, regulators became concerned about the vulnerability of the U.S. economy to increased dependence on foreign oil and responded with several policies, including energy price controls and regulations mandating improvements in automobile fuel efficiency. More recently, global climate change has been cited by advocates of regulations to increase fuel efficiency.

In many cases, the costs of these programs have outweighed their benefits to society. In some respects, the high cost was inevitable because the policy goals were conflicting. For example, control devices placed in motor vehicles to reduce smog-forming emissions have significant adverse effects on fuel efficiency. But the major, unnecessary shortcoming is that these policies rely on command-and-control measures rather than market incentives, an approach long recognized to have significantly reduced the cost-effectiveness of motor vehicle regulations.[59]

CONTROL OF MOTOR VEHICLE EMISSIONS

Since the early 1970s, new motor vehicles sold in the United States have had to meet progressively more stringent pollution control standards. As a consequence, emissions from new automobiles have declined dramatically.[60] However, the size of the motor vehicle fleet and the vehicle miles driven have increased significantly, offsetting some of these improvements, and motor vehicles remain an important source of pollution in urban areas.

Currently, the program for reducing motor vehicle emissions has three main components: (1) mandatory emission standards applied at the point of manufacture; (2) vehicle inspection and maintenance programs, which are mandatory in certain nonattainment areas, designed to prevent the deterioration of factory-installed controls; and (3) standards for fuels to be used, such as unleaded gasoline. The 1990 Clean Air Act Amendments will tighten standards in all these areas.

Motor Vehicle Emission Control Devices. The total cost of motor vehicle emission programs now in place and the added cost of the 1990 Amendments are difficult to estimate accurately but are undoubtedly very high. The OECD estimates, for example, that the added cost per vehicle of the three-way catalyst systems now used in automobiles ranges from 4 percent for high-priced vehicles to nearly 20 percent for less expensive vehicles.[61] The Bureau of Labor Statistics price data for new car quality improvements suggest that pollution control add-ons since model year 1968 have raised the average cost of new automobiles sold in the United States by an estimated $1,495 in 1990 dollars.[62] If that estimate is correct, and given the number of new motor vehicles sold (9.3 million in 1990), it implies a total *annual* cost to purchasers of almost $14 billion for pollution control equipment alone. The annual cost of the maintenance and inspection programs would add to that cost.

The emission control programs have resulted in a sharp decline in motor vehicle emissions, but the goal of achieving satisfactory urban ambient air quality has not been

---

*See memorandum by EDWIN LUPBERGER (page 95).

met in all places. As we pointed out in Chapter 2, unsatisfactory levels of ground ozone, the primary constituent of smog, remain a major problem in urban areas[63] (see "Motor Vehicle Emission Control and Urban Ozone," page 65). In October 1992, the EPA designated 97 areas as ozone nonattainment areas. Although the relative contribution of other emission sources has risen, motor vehicles still accounted for 23 percent of VOCs, 29 percent of NO_x, and 58 percent of CO emissions in the United States in 1991.[64]

The 1990 Amendments to the Clean Air Act attempted to deal with the motor vehicle's contribution to urban ozone by tightening emission standards further and requiring the use of reformulated gasoline, beginning in 1995, in nine urban areas with the worst ozone problems. Cost estimates for complying with Tier I emission controls vary widely, from a few hundred dollars to $1,600 per vehicle, reflecting the considerable range of uncertainty about the cost of these regulations.[65] The Office of Technology Assessment (OTA) puts the cost of new equipment on vehicles for nonattainment areas at $2 to $6 billion a year. When the cost for other regions is taken into consideration, that figure may double.[66] It is highly unlikely that these costs could be justified by benefit-cost analysis (see "Benefits and Costs of Programs to Reduce VOCs").

California has mandated new vehicle emission performance standards that are even more stringent than the federal regulations. The Low Emission Vehicle (LEV) standards are intended

---

MOTOR VEHICLE EMISSION CONTROL AND URBAN OZONE

The failure of the mobile and stationary emission control programs to solve urban ozone problems has been the subject of a great deal of recent study. Inadequate understanding of the factors influencing the process of local ozone creation has greatly hampered the formulation of fully effective regulatory strategies. A recent National Research Council study suggests that the failure to reduce ozone was caused in part by inadequate emission inventories and inaccurate estimates of volatile organic compounds (VOCs) emissions from both human activity and biogenic sources. It also found that the process by which VOCs and NO_x combine in sunlight to form ozone is more complicated and more dependent on local conditions than previously thought. The study indicates that the strategy used to abate urban ozone needs to be tailored to local conditions.[a] **CED agrees with the Council's proposal for a coordinated national research program directed at elucidating the chemical, physical, and meteorological processes that control ozone formation and concentrations over North America.**

(a) National Research Council, Committee on Tropospheric Ozone Formation and Measurement, *Rethinking the Ozone Problem in Urban and Regional Air Pollution* (Washington, DC: National Academy Press, 1992), pp. 1-16.

BENEFITS AND COSTS OF PROGRAMS TO REDUCE VOCS

A 1989 study by the Office of Technology Assessment estimated that with existing technology, the potential exists to achieve a 35 percent reduction nationwide in VOCs in nonattainment areas. A reduction of this size would equal approximately two-thirds of all reductions needed to allow nonattainment cities to meet the NAAQS. The nationwide cost of this program would be $8.8 to $13 billion annually in 2004.[a] By comparison, the short-term health benefits of fully achieving the standards for ozone are estimated to range between $0.5 and $4 billion annually, far below the cost.[b] This OTA study did not include the cost of reformulated gasoline for nonattainment areas or California.

(a) Costs attributable to automobile programs are estimated to be in the area of $8 billion. Office of Technology Assessment, *Catching Our Breath — Next Steps to Reducing Urban Ozone*, p. 141.

(b) Office of Technology Assessment, *Catching Our Breath—Next Steps to Reducing Urban Ozone*, pp. 9 and 13. For a summary explanation of such calculations, see Alan J. Krupnick and Paul R. Portney, "Controlling Urban Pollution: A Benefit-Cost Assessment," *Science* (April 1991): 522-527.

to address the unique air quality problems and operating conditions in southern California. Vehicle systems that are being designed to meet the LEV standard are being aided by California's stringent reformulated gasoline requirements. Meeting the California requirements will further increase the cost of new vehicles while achieving only marginal improvements in air quality above those generated by the Clean Air Act Amendments of 1990.

Reforms in the motor vehicle pollution abatement program to bring it in line with sound regulatory principles could significantly improve its cost-effectiveness. Present controls on new motor vehicles, for example, are not tied directly to the level of emissions created by a driver or to the damage created by the emissions, which varies from region to region. Because the emission abatement program is directed at the vehicle rather than at the emissions themselves, a salesperson who drives 100,000 miles per year may encounter the same control cost as a retired person who drives only a few miles each week. Moreover, uniform national control systems, which place the same financial burden on vehicles in all areas (except California), may not reduce emissions sufficiently in some congested nonattainment areas, although they may provide limited benefits in rural areas.

The pollution abatement devices required for new automobiles have also raised the price of these vehicles relative to older ones. This appears to have contributed to the rising average age of the vehicle fleet.[67] A large number of local and state governments also impose personal property taxes (or similar fees) on vehicles registered in the area.[68] Because the fee is generally based on market value, owners of newer automobiles pay a high fee (often exceeding $1,000), which also encourages motorists to retain old, "dirty" cars. These effects are important because pre-1981 passenger vehicles account for 71 percent of all vehicle hydrocarbon (HC) emissions, even though they make up only 30 percent of the fleet and account for an even lower percentage of miles driven. These older vehicles are said

to produce three times more hydrocarbons, two times more NO_x, and eight times more CO per mile driven than new vehicles.[69] Thus, the motor vehicle pollution abatement program and other policies (including CAFE standards) that encourage the aging of the fleet have an adverse effect on urban smog.

CED opposes requiring additional improvements in new vehicle emissions performance beyond those set out in the Clean Air Act Amendments of 1990 until we gain experience with the present law. CED opposes the extension of California's vehicle and fuel requirements to other states unless these requirements can be shown to pass a cost-benefit test and to be cost-effective relative to other strategies to meet ambient air quality standards.

Reformulated Gasoline. Title II of the 1990 Clean Air Act Amendments mandated new specifications for reformulated gasoline starting in 1995 in the nine urban areas with the worst ozone problems.[70] In addition, regulations have been put in place in California that are far more stringent than the federal standards in order to address California's unique air quality problems. There is considerable uncertainty about the cost of reformulated fuels, and these costs are likely to change along with refining process technology. Furthermore, as vehicle emissions control systems become more complex and expensive, more extensive control of fuel characteristics becomes relatively more cost-effective. In general, however, more stringent reformulation provides smaller incremental benefits at higher cost than less stringent reformulation. Reformulated gasolines that meet the 1990 Clean Air Act are estimated by the EPA to cost between $2,000 and $4,000 per ton of VOCs reduced. The California Air Resource Board has estimated that the cost of reformulated gasoline proposed for California could be between $8,000 and $12,000 per ton of VOC reduced. Some industry estimates are much higher. These cost estimates greatly exceed OTA 1989 estimates of the benefits of meeting ambient ozone standards, which are in the range of $200 to $600 per ton of VOCs reduced. Moreover, the costs could rise if additional states adopt the reformulated gasoline program.

One estimate places the eventual capital cost at some $30 billion.[71] The cost to consumers has been estimated at $0.05 to $0.10 per gallon by the mid-1990s and perhaps as much as $0.20 to $0.25 per gallon after 1997 for stringent reformulations.[72]

Because reformulated gasoline would be consumed by vehicles of all ages, its impact on the atmosphere would be quick. However, there is a great deal of uncertainty about the process by which smog is created. While it is clear that some benefits from reductions in emissions will accrue, it is unclear how much improvement will occur because of these fuels. More important, it is doubtful that the benefits of mandated reformulated fuels are commensurate with their costs even in California, and this is certainly true in most areas outside California. **CED opposes the extension of California standards beyond California. CED also opposes the extension of federal reformulated gasoline requirements beyond the nine cities already affected unless costs can be shown to be in line with potential benefits.**

Alternative Fuels. At the moment, there is considerable uncertainty associated with the use of alternative fuels such as methanol, ethanol, electricity, and natural gas in motor vehicles. These uncertainties revolve around cost, performance, and emission characteristics. Some of these fuels may have the potential to reduce mobile source emissions of ozone precursors, and it is feasible that technical advances will eventually make one or more price-competitive with gasoline. However, a recent National Research Council (NRC) study concluded that "requiring the widespread use of any specific fuel would be premature" because there is uncertainty about the degree to which alternative fuels would reduce ozone.[73] Current research has also failed to identify a clear front-runner in terms of costs and emission reductions, though some options appear to be prohibitively expensive.[74] **CED supports federal funding of research and development into promising alternative fuels.**

However, we oppose mandating the introduction of given numbers of alternatively fueled vehicles, as in the Clean Air Act of 1990 and the 1992 energy bill. The latter requirement is a highly inefficient means of reducing urban pollution because, like CAFE standards, it imposes high costs on manufacturers and targets only new vehicles, and therefore, it would affect emissions very slowly. Furthermore, because of their high cost, mandated alternative fuels would also encourage retention of old vehicles.

It is also important to understand the objectives of using alternative fuels and evaluate the environmental effects of specific fuels over the entire fuel cycle rather than simply in the final combustion process. For example, electric vehicles may reduce emissions of ozone precursors, but if these vehicles simultaneously lead to an increase in emissions from utilities that generate the power to recharge the batteries, they may not represent a solution to local pollution or GHG emissions.

MOTOR VEHICLE EMISSION CHARGES AND ACCELERATED RETIREMENT OF OLD VEHICLES

The current program for controlling motor vehicle emissions has not been cost-effective in part because of its reliance on inefficient technology-based control measures. Consequently, CED believes that policy makers should shift emphasis to market-based control mechanisms, such as emission charges and incentives to accelerate retirement of old vehicles.

Emission Charges. The 1990 Amendments to the Clean Air Act mandate change in automobile technology and reformulated fuels in certain urban areas in order to bring these areas into compliance with air quality standards. The cost of this program is expected to be very high. Time will be needed to assess the effects of this legislation, although the EPA expects this program to sharply reduce the contribution of the automobile to urban pollution. However, if further motor vehicle emission controls are deemed to be appropriate, **CED believes that instead of mandating con-**

tinuously more costly technology-based emission controls, consideration should be given to the development of a cost-effective emission charge program to control pollution from motor vehicles. Although an emission charge could efficiently lower pollution, the potentially high administrative costs and adverse income distribution impacts of such a program need to be clarified. As discussed in Chapter 3, emission controls directed at the technology of a product rather than at emissions themselves are not likely to be the most cost-effective instrument. By comparison, an emission charge would create the correct incentives. The lower charge for cleaner vehicles would encourage the purchase and maintenance of low-emission vehicles and discourage the retention of older "dirty" cars. With such charges, vehicle owners would have an incentive to maintain emission control equipment on vehicles. Drivers would be penalized according to the emissions they create, thereby providing an incentive to reduce activity that generates emissions. CED also recommends that state and local governments consider replacing personal property and other motor vehicle taxes that encourage the aging of the fleet with charges on emissions.

An emission charge program would require an annual registration and inspection, at which time each vehicle would be rated on emissions (grams per mile). The vehicle owner would be required to pay an emission charge based on this rating and total miles driven.[75] The charge could be higher for vehicles registered in nonattainment areas. Some believe that with modern technology, it would also be possible to have a system of variable emission charges that increase during smog alerts or during the time of day when ozone levels are highest.[76] An advantage of an emission charge program is that it would require that present inspection programs be improved. The failure of inspection programs to require maintenance of emission control equipment means that the benefits of improved vehicles are often not being realized. CED supports the EPA's recent efforts to improve existing inspection programs.

Although moving regulation away from mandatory engineering controls on vehicles toward a tax on emissions would create the right economic incentives for reducing emissions, some fear that the additional administrative costs of such a program would be quite high. Currently, federal law mandates inspection programs in about 180 cities in 37 states. About an equal number of states have some form of tax on motor vehicles. An emission charge program need not be significantly more costly than these inspection and tax programs. The emission charges could make motor vehicle pollution abatement programs much more effective.

One shortcoming of emission charges on motor vehicles is that they fall heavily on older cars, many of which are owned by individuals with low incomes. One way to minimize the impact on lower-income individuals is to combine the emission charges with an accelerated vehicle retirement program.

Accelerated Retirement of Old Vehicles. The relatively high emission rates and low fuel efficiency of older motor vehicles have led to a number of proposals for retiring older, higher-polluting vehicles. Because lower-income households own proportionately more older vehicles, mandatory retirement of these vehicles could place a large burden on low-income families.[77] However, the problem of regressivity could be addressed by paying a bounty for old vehicles to compensate their owners. The Unocal Corporation experimented with a limited program in 1990 in southern California in which it purchased pre-1971 vehicles for $700.[78] The cost per ton of HC removed is thought to be fairly high; however, such programs could deliver large savings if the scrappage program generated marketable emission credits (for the vehicle purchased) that could be used to reduce the cost of complying with other emission requirements. In this way, society would benefit by permitting the substitution of lower-cost mobile source emission reductions from early retirement of vehicles for more expensive reductions from rigid command-and-control regulations on other emission sources.

An accelerated scrappage program sponsored by government has also been proposed as an alternative to increases in the CAFE standards for the purpose of reducing gasoline consumption and pollution. A study undertaken by DRI/McGraw-Hill, which assumed that a gasoline tax of $0.02 per gallon would be used to finance the program, found that a scrappage program would be a more effective instrument for reducing hydrocarbons, NO_x, and CO than raising CAFE to 32 miles per gallon over a four-year period.[79] The scrappage program also would produce a significant reduction in CO_2.

CED recommends the development of a scrappage program whereby owners of high-polluting vehicles in nonattainment areas would be offered a bounty for their vehicles. We believe that a scrappage program could deliver large savings if firms receive marketable emission permits (for purchasing the vehicles) that can be used to comply with other emission requirements.

CAFE

Following the 1973 OPEC oil embargo, the public became concerned about increasing U.S. dependence on foreign oil. With the price of petroleum products controlled below market levels, many felt that conservation should be encouraged with nonprice mechanisms. When Congress enacted the Energy Policy and Conservation Act of 1975, it placed particular emphasis on auto fuel economy because the transportation sector accounts for a large share of petroleum consumption and because of the visibility of the automotive sector. This legislation required that the corporate average fuel economy (CAFE) for new cars be raised gradually from 14.2 miles per gallon in model year 1974 to 27.5 miles per gallon by model year 1985.[80] The required increase in CAFE was eventually achieved, but this improvement in fuel efficiency may have been as much a result of gasoline prices as of CAFE.[81]

Despite the improvement in motor vehicle efficiency, gasoline consumption has increased in the United States, and our dependence on foreign oil supplies has risen.[82] However, concern about our dependence on foreign oil appears to have diminished because of the creation of the Strategic Petroleum Reserve, the growing diversity of energy sources, and the global nature of the petroleum market. The experience of the recent Persian Gulf conflict, when petroleum production from two major oil producers (Kuwait and Iraq) was completely disrupted without major economic consequences, seems to have further allayed fears about U.S. dependence. Nevertheless, increased CAFE remains a popular goal of regulators, though proponents now most frequently cite the problem of global climate change.

CAFE and Gasoline Consumption. Since 1972, the average fuel economy of new domestic automobiles has increased more than 100 percent. The gain in CAFE was achieved by reducing the weight of automobiles, improving engine and drivetrain efficiency, reducing tire rolling resistance, and improving the aerodynamics of design. But gasoline consumption by automobiles did not decline sharply and the combined consumption of automobiles and trucks has continued to grow (see Table 8, page 71).

Why has CAFE not been a more effective instrument for reducing gasoline consumption? The answer is that the fuel efficiency of new automobiles is only one of many determinants of gasoline consumption. The three major factors influencing fuel consumption are: (1) the number of vehicles in the fleet, (2) average miles driven per vehicle and changes in the proportion of total miles driven by large vehicles and by more fuel-efficient small vehicles, and (3) the average vehicle fuel efficiency (miles per gallon) of the entire fleet, including trucks. CAFE directly affects only the third determinant, which can be overwhelmed by the first two. Indeed, between 1970 and 1991, the car population rose more than 60 percent and trucks, which get substantially fewer miles per gallon, by 128 percent. This growth appears to have been driven mainly by demographics, vehicle prices, and consumer incomes. The second factor, average vehicle miles driven, has also risen, particularly for trucks (see Table 8). The shift in consumer preference toward light trucks has had an important impact on gasoline consumption. The total number of vehicle miles travelled (VMT) appears to be heavily influenced by gasoline prices (see Figure 41).

The price of gasoline also appears to affect the average miles per gallon through its influence on consumer preferences for fuel-efficient cars (see Figure 42) and on decisions by two-car families to drive the more fuel-efficient vehicle.

Even if other factors did not moderate its influence, CAFE could not affect gasoline consumption quickly. CAFE *directly* improves miles per gallon of *new* vehicles only. The impact on the fuel economy of the entire fleet occurs very slowly, as older vehicles are scrapped. Today, the average fuel economy for the entire fleet is around 21 miles per gallon, still well below the requirement for new vehicles.

In evaluating the effects of CAFE on the nation's fuel consumption, it is also important to recognize two counterproductive effects: (1) CAFE encourages increased driving because it lowers the cost of vehicle miles travelled; (2) CAFE encourages the retention of old, low-mileage vehicles because it adds substantially to the cost of new vehicles.[83]

In short, the effectiveness of CAFE as a measure to reduce gasoline consumption has been limited by the fact that the regulation is directed at motor vehicle efficiency, rather than at fuel consumption itself.*

CAFE and the Environment. Sometimes higher CAFE standards have been advocated as a means of reducing urban pollution. However, urban smog does not appear to be very closely related to motor vehicle fuel efficiency. CAFE-induced improvements would lower CO_2 emissions, but HC, CO, and NO_x would not be substantially affected, according to the NRC, because emission regulations control grams per mile driven rather than grams per gallon.[84] Moreover, by reducing its cost, CAFE encourages driving, an activity that increases emissions. Thus, the cost of increased CAFE would be well above any likely benefit derived from improved local air quality.

Today, proponents of increased CAFE usually indicate that their purpose is to reduce gasoline consumption in order to decrease emissions of CO_2. But CAFE is not the most cost-effective way to reduce gasoline consumption because it is directed at fuel efficiency rather than use. Moreover, CAFE is not a cost-effective instrument for reducing CO_2 because motor vehicle fuel consumption in the United States accounts for only a small fraction of worldwide CO_2 emissions. The relative ineffectiveness of CAFE in reducing CO_2 emissions has been confirmed in recent studies (see "The Cost-Effectiveness of CAFE and Other Instruments to Reduce CO_2").

The Cost of Increased CAFE. Although CAFE's environmental benefits appear quite limited, there remains considerable interest in legislation to require substantial further improvements in the fuel efficiency of new motor vehicles. Although proposals for increased CAFE have recently been rejected

---

THE COST-EFFECTIVENESS OF CAFE AND OTHER INSTRUMENTS TO REDUCE CO_2

A study recently published by Charles River Associates compared the cost-effectiveness of a CAFE standard of 40 miles per gallon with several other options to achieve the same reduction in CO_2. It confirmed that market incentives with the broadest possible coverage have the greatest potential for yielding the least-cost ways of reducing energy use and lowering CO_2 emissions.[a] The study compared the cost-effectiveness of CAFE, gasoline taxes, oil taxes, and a carbon tax for reducing CO_2 emissions. The results were that a 40-mpg CAFE would be many times more expensive than the lowest-cost policies. The cost of a gasoline tax was about one-quarter of the cost of CAFE. But a carbon tax is by far the most effective instrument, according to the study. The study also found that transportation management policies and some alternative fuels are likely to be more cost-effective than increases in CAFE.

(a) Charles River Associates, Inc., *Policy Alternatives for Reducing Petroleum Use and Greenhouse Gas Emissions* (Boston, MA: CRA, September 1991).

---

*See memorandum by ROCCO C. SICILIANO (page 95).

Table 8

U.S. Gasoline Consumption, 1970 to 1991

	1970	1975	1980	1985	1991
Gasoline Consumption (million barrels per day)					
Cars	**4.4**	**5.0**	**4.7**	**4.5**	**4.5**
Trucks	**1.1**	**1.5**	**1.9**	**2.3**	**2.7**
Total	**5.5**	**6.5**	**6.6**	**6.8**	**7.2**
AverageVehicle Miles Travelled/Yr (thousands)					
Cars	**10.3**	**9.7**	**9.1**	**9.6**	**10.6**
Trucks	**8.7**	**9.8**	**10.4**	**11.0**	**12.1**
Vehicle Efficiency (miles per gallon)					
New cars	**14.2**	**15.8**	**24.3**	**27.6**	**28.2**
All cars	**13.5**	**13.5**	**15.5**	**18.2**	**20.9**
Vehicle Population (millions)					
Cars	**89.2**	**106.7**	**121.7**	**132.1**	**145.0**
Trucks	**18.8**	**25.8**	**33.6**	**39.6**	**45.7**

SOURCE: Motor Vehicle Manufacturers Association and Energy Information Administration

Figure 41

Gasoline Price Versus Vehicle Miles Travelled, 1974-89

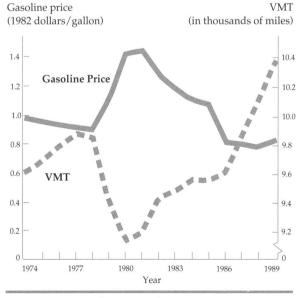

SOURCE: Energy Information Administration

Figure 42

Market Share of Subcompact Cars Versus Gasoline Prices, 1974-89

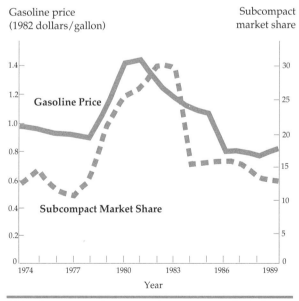

SOURCE: Energy Information Administration and *Ward's Automotive Yearbook*

by Congress, political pressures for mandatory increases remain. Policy makers need to know: (1) whether large increases in CAFE are technically feasible and at what cost and (2) whether increased CAFE is the most cost-effective means of achieving its objective.

An NRC study, published in 1992, indicates that further gains in fuel economy are "technically achievable" but at a great cost that could exceed the value of the gasoline saved. The NRC estimates with "high confidence" that by model year 2006, it would be technically possible for passenger cars to achieve improvements in miles per gallon in the range of 16 to 28 percent (depending on size class) at a cost ranging from $500 to $1,250 per vehicle. Projections of larger gains, ranging from 30 to 40 percent and costing about $2,500 per vehicle, were made with "lower confidence."[85]

The study cites additional nonmonetary costs involving increased emissions, reduced performance, less room and comfort for passengers, and possibly, reduced vehicle safety.[86] Because consumers seem to value comfort and performance very highly, the demand for vehicles that are much more fuel efficient may be very weak. The NRC stated that at the current level of gasoline prices, consumers do not consider fuel economy an important priority in the decision to purchase new vehicles.[87] The positive correlation between gasoline prices and the demand for fuel-efficient cars was demonstrated in the 1980s, when consumer demand shifted to larger, less fuel-efficient vehicles as the price of gasoline declined.

Another drawback of CAFE is that it has an adverse effect on the competitiveness of U.S. manufacturers. Since fuel economy tends to be greater for small cars, those manufacturers that primarily sell small cars can more easily meet the standards than full-line manufacturers. As a result, importers of small cars have been able to move into large car market segments with little constraint, while the regulations limit incremental large car sales by the domestic manufacturers. This system has operated to the benefit of Japanese producers at the expense of U.S. manufacturers.[88]

Further, the CAFE regulations require that for each manufacturer, domestic and import fleets meet the standard separately. A domestically assembled unit is treated as an import if its import content exceeds a given threshold. Now that the Japanese are exporting larger cars to the United States, they have an incentive to limit domestic content of transplant production so that the small cars produced in the United States will be treated as imports and averaged with their import fleet.[89]

Taking all these factors into consideration, CED believes that the benefits to society of increased CAFE would be small, certainly far below its costs. Therefore, we oppose an increase in CAFE.

GASOLINE TAXES

CED supports the principle of imposing additional taxes on the consumption of products that demonstrably impose external health, safety, and environmental costs which exceed current levels of taxation.[90] Increased taxes that reflect "external costs," which are not included in the prices paid by consumers and producers but are borne instead by other members of society, may actually improve the efficiency of resource allocation. Such product taxes can also generate substantial revenues for government and are sometimes recommended because of their combined environmental and fiscal effects. Proponents of increased gasoline taxes, in particular, have argued that this tax is administratively simple and would address air pollution, the trade imbalance, and the federal budget deficit all at once.

As an Environmental Measure. If the nation's ultimate goal were only to reduce fuel consumption by motor vehicles, which it is not, the principles of sound regulation would indicate that higher gasoline taxes would be the most cost-effective instrument. Gasoline taxes impinge directly on fuel consumption and therefore discourage driving and encourage the purchase of fuel-efficient vehicles, which suggests that they would achieve a given reduction in gasoline consumption at a lower cost than CAFE.[91]

ECONOMIC CONSEQUENCES OF GASOLINE TAXES

All regulations and taxes, such as CAFE and gasoline taxes, place a burden on society that is justified only if the benefits exceed the costs. Opponents of gasoline taxes are particularly concerned about the distributional effects and the effects on the economy.[a] In the short run, newly imposed burdens can have significant cyclical effects on employment and output. These short-run effects reflect changes in consumers' discretionary spending and shifts in industry demand. However, major disruptions to the overall economy can normally be avoided if the changes are small relative to the economy and are phased in slowly. But the longer-run adverse effects on economic growth cannot be avoided. This is one reason why it is critical that environmental and other regulatory policies be as efficient as possible.

Proponents of a gasoline tax argue that the long-run economic effects would be small because a gasoline tax would improve the U.S. balance of trade. They also argue that a gasoline tax would improve economic efficiency by internalizing the external costs of fuel consumption. Both of these arguments are disputed. The U.S. trade imbalance is generally viewed as a macroeconomic problem, the consequence of low national saving and relatively strong domestic demand for capital. On the question of social costs of gasoline consumption, some economists, such as Michael Boskin, the former Chairman of the Council of Economic Advisers, believe that the taxes currently imposed on gasoline by all levels of government (about $0.35 per gallon) already internalize all social costs.[b]

(a) Norman B. Ture et al. *The Impact, Shifting and Incidence of an Increase in the Gasoline Excise Tax* (Washington, DC: Institute for Research on the Economics of Taxation, April 1992).

(b) Boskin presented this case to the NRC committee on July 10, 1991. National Research Council, *Automotive Fuel Economy: How Far Should We Go?* p. 25.

However, our interest is in improving air quality, not in gasoline consumption per se. Although a gasoline tax would discourage fuel consumption and thereby reduce emissions, it would not be the most cost-effective instrument for reducing either local pollution or CO_2 emissions. An efficient environmental control mechanism would apply to emissions rather than products. Therefore, a motor vehicle emission charge would be more effective in dealing with local pollution from mobile sources.[92] Moreover, a gasoline tax would not be a cost-effective way to deal with global climate change. The transportation sector accounts for about 25 percent of U.S. emissions of GHGs, and gasoline-powered light vehicles account for about 57 percent of GHGs generated by the U.S. transportation sector. CO_2 emissions attributable to highway transportation in the United States are believed to be responsible for as little as 2.3 percent of the human contribution to GHGs worldwide. Clearly, there is little rationale for choosing this one source for special treatment. An efficient and effective program for reducing GHGs must be aimed at a broad range of sources, which explains why a carbon tax would be a much more effective instrument for reducing CO_2 emissions.

Advocates of a higher gasoline tax frequently argue that it would improve economic efficiency by internalizing the social costs of gasoline consumption. However, some recent studies have found that existing gasoline taxes already internalize the cost of local air pollution.[92] Moreover, the regulations imposed by the Clean Air Act of 1990 are expected to sharply reduce the motor vehicle contribution to urban pollution, leaving less room for additional benefits from gasoline taxes. Indeed, the costs of the 1990 Clean Air Act with respect to automotive fuel and vehicle emission controls are expected to greatly exceed the benefits of reduced emissions.

CED concludes that although it is appropriate to impose taxes on fuels in order to internalize the social costs of consuming them, existing taxes on gasoline and other pending regulations may already cover the

effects on local pollution. Moreover, a gasoline tax is not the most cost-effective instrument for controlling CO_2 emissions. For these reasons, CED does not support increased gasoline taxes solely as an environmental measure.

As a Combined Fiscal and Environmental Measure. The combined federal, state, and local tax on gasoline in the United States averages about $0.35 per gallon, far below the tax imposed in most other advanced industrial countries (see Figure 15, page 20). Most countries use the gasoline tax as a major source of government revenues. Many analysts believe that increased federal taxes on gasoline are an attractive option for the United States because of the combination of favorable fiscal and environmental effects.

Higher taxes would contribute to improved air quality because they would discourage gasoline consumption. The magnitude of the reduction would depend on the size of the tax increase and the responsiveness of consumers to price changes. It is generally believed that the demand for gasoline is relatively inelastic in the short run because it is difficult for consumers to adjust behavior quickly. But over time, the demand for gasoline would respond more strongly to price changes because consumers would have an opportunity to alter their behavior and to gradually replace existing vehicles with more fuel-efficient models.

Gasoline taxes are also viewed by some as an administratively simple revenue source to help lower the budget deficit and as an instrument for reducing U.S. dependence on foreign oil. Because gasoline taxes fall on consumption rather than on saving or investment, some argue that increases would probably do less harm to the international competitiveness of U.S. industry than many other possible revenue sources. In addition, it is argued that since most other nations now impose much higher gasoline taxes than the United States does, some increase would still leave U.S. producers at a competitive advantage with respect to gasoline costs.

All taxes distort the allocation of resources and represent a burden on the private economy, though broad-based taxes generally are less burdensome than narrowly based excise taxes, such as a gasoline tax. However, economic efficiency can be improved by taxes and other regulations that internalize the social costs of consumption. Just as the social cost of alcohol and tobacco consumption can be reduced by taxes on these products, additional taxes on gasoline can ameliorate the costs to society of the adverse external effects of its consumption on the environment, economic security, or urban congestion.[93] Thus, in the judgment of some, gasoline taxes are less burdensome, on balance, than many other taxes that do not have these favorable social effects.

CED does not recommend increased gasoline taxes purely as an environmental measure because a gasoline tax would not be as cost-effective as other instruments for dealing either with urban pollution or with global climate change. The issue of gasoline taxes as a fiscal measure is beyond the scope of this paper. Before CED would take a position on the merits of a gasoline tax as a fiscal instrument, it would be necessary to undertake a comprehensive evaluation of alternative fiscal measures, including broad-based tax options (such as a value-added tax or a national sales tax) and broad-based energy taxes. It would also be necessary to compare with other fiscal measures the impact of gasoline taxes on consumers (on a national and regional basis), on the international competitiveness position of the United States, and on the environment.

NUCLEAR ENERGY

Advanced industrial nations have invested heavily in nuclear power to generate electricity. Although the initial projections of the cost of nuclear power have proved to be too optimistic and concerns about safety have heightened, many nations still find it attractive and continue its expansion. In the United States, however, concerns about safety, waste disposal, and costs have sharply reduced the future prospects for nuclear energy. However, the industry could be rescued by major regulatory reform and improved technology, particularly if concern about global climate change increases.

Most forecasters anticipate rising demand for electricity over the next 20 years.[94] The likelihood of increasing demand and apprehension about the environment mean that important decisions will need to be made by policy makers and utility planners concerning the future energy mix. The principal criterion for these decisions will be the comparative cost-effectiveness of different fuels. Nuclear energy becomes a more attractive option if the externalities related to burning coal, oil, and other conventional fuels are fully taken into account. The competitiveness of nuclear energy will also be influenced by the costs of renewable energy and taxes on fossil fuels.

THE NUCLEAR POWER INDUSTRY TODAY

Today, nuclear power accounts for nearly 22 percent of U.S. electricity generation. However, no new plants have been ordered since 1978, and the existing capital stock is aging. A nuclear plant receives an operating license for 40 years, and over 50 percent of the 109 plants in the United States are threatened with closure by 2020 unless the utilities that own them apply for and are granted life extensions.[95]

To the extent that it is necessary to retire existing plants, nuclear power's share of U.S. electricity generation will diminish unless new plants are built. But prospects for building a new generation of nuclear plants are dogged by the indifferent performance of the industry with respect to both economics and safety. Building nuclear plants has become a very expensive proposition, and on average, the cost of electricity produced by nuclear power (operation and maintenance plus fuel) now exceeds that of coal-fired plants (see Table 9).

Two critical questions about nuclear power must be answered: (1) Do the cost trends for nuclear power have predictive value for the future, in light of current and potential reform of the design, licensing, construction, and operation processes? (2) How will environmental issues affect decisions concerning

Table 9		
Electricity Production Costs[a]		
1990 cents per kilowatt-hour		
	1981	1990
Nuclear	**1.61**	**2.19**
Coal	**2.72**	**2.02**
Gas	**4.59**	**3.11**
Oil	**7.38**	**4.08**

(a) Includes operations, maintenance, and fuel costs. Excludes capital costs.

SOURCE: U.S. Council for Energy Awareness, citing Utility Data Institute.

nuclear power? **In CED's view, decisions on the cost-effectiveness of conventional fossil fuels, nuclear energy, renewable energy sources, and energy efficiency should be based on a comparison of the full social costs of each option, including costs to the environment and other externalities.[96]**

Public Attitudes. It is frequently argued that nuclear energy has no future because the public believes it is not safe. However, some polling data suggest that nuclear power may be gaining ground in public opinion because of escalating environmental concerns about the continued use of fossil fuels.[97] Public wariness is founded on anxieties about safety problems (real and imagined) in the construction and operation of nuclear facilities and on the failure to find a permanent solution to the problem of nuclear waste disposal. After Three Mile Island, the Institute of Nuclear Power Operations (INPO) was created to police the industry and promulgate best-practice standards. INPO has been credited with considerable success in its mission, demonstrating that the pressure of peer review can have a very beneficial effect.[98] Following the successful pattern established by INPO, the world's nuclear community responded to the 1986 Chernobyl accident by forming the World Association of Nuclear Operators (WANO) in May 1989.

The Utilities' Perspective. Public opposition is only one source of resistance to nuclear power. The utilities themselves are loathe to buy into a technology plagued by regulatory uncertainty and rising costs. No one is willing to invest $3 billion in a plant that could take more than 12 years to build and then perhaps not receive an operating license. The prohibitive cost of building plants is reinforced by the rapid growth of operation and maintenance costs that occurred throughout the 1980s and by the cost of capital additions made after operations have begun. (The costs of such additions escalated rapidly in the first half of the 1980s as a result of regulatory activity and industry self-improvement initiatives but have since declined as major programs have been implemented).[99]

Environmental and Other Benefits. Only when utilities are convinced that costs can be controlled and plants operated economically, and only when the public is assured that plants can be operated safely, will the expansion of nuclear power become feasible again.

The challenges are significant, and there is great political pressure to wind down the nuclear industry. However, there is also increasing concern about the link between combustion of fossil fuels and global warming. Electricity generated by nuclear power produces no CO_2, SO_2, or NO_x pollutants associated with global warming, acid rain, and urban smog. Moreover, the contribution of nuclear power to U.S. electricity generation during the past 20 years has significantly displaced that of imported oil. One study estimates that during the period from 1973 to 1990, nuclear energy in the United States reduced oil consumption by a cumulative total of 4.6 billion barrels (somewhat more than two years of imports at 1990 levels). The environmental benefits of using nuclear energy instead of fossil fuel alternatives were estimated at 42 million tons of reduced emissions of SO_2, 18 million tons less NO_x, and 4,600 million tons less CO_2.[100] **CED believes these are compelling reasons to explore options for improving the cost-effectiveness and safety of nuclear power so that it can be retained as an option for generating electricity.**

Nuclear power is now a mature technology

with considerable learning experience and infrastructure. If this human and capital infrastructure is lost and the nuclear option is found to be necessary again in the future, the United States could be beholden to foreign sources of plant and expertise. Finally, in an era of intense concern about proliferation, it is possible that U.S. abandonment of its nuclear industry would vitiate our influence over nuclear issues in international forums and reduce our leverage over the movement of nuclear technology between countries.

Safety of Existing Reactors. New institutional arrangements are likely to be necessary if more nuclear plants are to be built in this country. However, we should not overlook the fact that safe operation of existing facilities is critical to their prospects for license renewal and to the prospects of successfully commercializing new reactors.[101] **Although regulatory oversight is important, the nuclear power industry must continue to police itself vigorously. Poor performers should be pressured to live up to the high standards that the industry sets for itself.**

Industry policing out of self-interest can help to ensure that U.S. nuclear plants are run safely and efficiently. However, many plants in other countries, particularly in Eastern Europe and the former Soviet Union, have deficiencies in design and operation that hold greater potential for serious accidents. Another accident such as that at Chernobyl in 1986 could further undermine public confidence here in the United States, even though the light-water reactor technology at U.S. facilities is superior to that of the Soviet-designed plants. With safety as their first priority, all 31 countries that operate nuclear power programs now participate in WANO. Members cooperate in the exchange of operating experience, the sharing of good practices, and an operator-to-operator exchange program. This multinational effort has enhanced safe and cost-effective nuclear plant operation at both domestic and foreign plants.

In August 1992, the U.S. government agreed to purchase highly enriched uranium from dismantled Russian warheads. The agreement included a provision that part of the proceeds be used by Russia to upgrade its unsafe reactors. Specific terms of the contract are being negotiated, and it is uncertain how much money will actually be available for reactor improvement.[102] **We urge the U.S. government and nuclear industry to take an interest in the improvement of safety at nuclear plants in all countries where high standards of construction and operation have not been observed. At a minimum, this should involve technical assistance.**

THE REGULATORY FRAMEWORK

All commercial nuclear plants operating in the United States today underwent a two-step licensing process: (1) a construction permit issued prior to commencement of work and (2) an operating license issued after construction was completed. Both licenses were granted only after formal hearings with public participation. The industry was new, and nuclear plants were designed and built in an evolving regulatory and technological environment. It was common for construction permits to be issued on the basis of an incomplete design (less than 15 percent in many instances),[103] with problems being solved as construction proceeded. This meant that regulatory standards were also introduced in a "regulate as you go" manner. This process created great uncertainty about ultimate construction costs and schedules. Moreover, sufficient information to evaluate whether a plant was safe to operate became available only after construction was completed, with billions of dollars already invested by the utilities. Hearings on the issuance of operating licenses tended to be long and vitriolic, causing delays in plant start-up at further cost to the utilities.

Construction Times and Capital Costs. The steady accumulation of regulations introduced over the life of the U.S. nuclear industry has improved plant safety, but it has also had an increasingly sinister effect on construction times. In the 1960s and early 1970s, construction of U.S. plants averaged about five and a half years, on a par with times in other industrialized countries. However, U.S. plants that entered service in the 1980s took twice as long to build. In the meantime, the French, Japanese, and West Germans had experienced only small increases in construction times.[104]

Drawn out construction times are pernicious because they add to costs, especially through increased financing charges, and also through the rising cost of labor and building materials. Moreover, because the regulatory environment has been constantly changing, longer construction times have increased vulnerability to unforeseen regulatory action involving costly capital additions or modifications.

This process explains in large part why nuclear plants have been much more expensive to build than had been expected. According to a Department of Energy analysis that compared capital carrying charges for nuclear and coal plants, nuclear is on average three times more costly.[105] The rate of return on investment in nuclear power has also been adversely affected. Most plants built since the second half of the 1970s have been sold to utilities on a cost-plus rather than a fixed-price basis. Utilities that incurred big construction cost overruns would have originally expected to be able to pass these costs on to their customers. However, the state utility commissions responsible for setting electricity rates have not been so generous. As a result of so-called prudency reviews, costs have frequently been passed backward to the utility stockholders rather than forward to the consumers. During the 1980s, some $13.8 billion was disallowed by utility commissions, over half of which was attributable to managerial imprudence in engineering, construction, and scheduling. Such disallowances will therefore act as a major disincentive to investment in new nuclear plants unless there is greater certainty that construction costs will come in within budget.[106]

It was perceived that much of the uncertainty about construction costs and time horizons was avoidable if plant designs were sufficiently complete before beginning construction so that all safety questions could be resolved in advance, and a combined construction and operating license issued on the basis of these designs.[107] The Energy Policy Act of 1992 codified combined licensing into the law.

Standardization. Combined licensing represents a positive step in creating appropriate conditions for the construction of new nuclear plants. Moreover, the creation of a small number of standardized reactor designs could speed licensing and construction and reduce costs. It would also lend itself to standardization of operation and maintenance and create a number of other economies.[108]

The U.S. nuclear industry is now moving in this direction. Four advanced light-water reactor (ALWR) designs are currently in the Nuclear Regulatory Commission (NRC) certification process: two large (1,300 megawatts of electricity, or MWe) and two midsize reactors (600 MWe).[109] The large ALWRs, referred to as "evolutionary," incorporate the best design features of the most recently constructed nuclear reactors and some technological improvements that enhance safety and ease of operation. The midsize ALWRs incorporate passive safety features, such as the use of gravity and convection, that reduce the amount of piping, control cable, pumps, and other items which must be activated in a conventional reactor. The NRC expects to be able to certify these reactor designs by 1996. The designs would then be "usable for a multiple number of units or at a multiple number of sites without reopening or repeating NRC licensing review."[110]

The evolutionary and passive-safety light-water reactors are not the only advanced reactor designs currently under development, but they are the closest to design maturity.[111] Deployment of the reactors may be possible early in the next decade.[112]

With the advent of standardized plants, the patchwork of regulations that evolved over the years to address design and construction problems will need to be reassessed. **The Nuclear Regulatory Commission should review its regulations for their applicability to standardized ALWRs.**

Operation and Maintenance. Nuclear plant operation and maintenance (O&M) costs per kilowatt of capacity increased about 90 percent in real terms during the 1980s.[113] On average, production costs at nuclear plants exceed those at coal-fired plants. Increased regulatory activity is cited as a major contributor to escalating O&M costs at nuclear plants. Other factors include utility actions to improve plant performance and reduce downtime (including more staff and staff training programs) and plant aging.

A positive outcome of these greater expenditures is their contribution to the performance of nuclear plants, which has progressed markedly during the last decade. The average capacity factor (ratio of actual output to maximum potential output) of U.S. plants reached 70.2 in 1991, an industry record.[114] Other performance indicators such as the number of "scrams" (unplanned automatic reactor shutdowns) and cases of radiation exposure have also shown improvement. Better management practices, encouraged particularly by the activities of INPO and WANO, have also made a significant contribution to these improvements. In France, standardization of plant designs has provided an opportunity to standardize operation, maintenance, and staff training and procedures. The U.S. nuclear industry believes that such "standardization beyond design" can be emulated in this country and that it will create efficiencies which enhance safety and cost-effectiveness.[115]

It is possible that standardization of designs will not create ideal conditions for continuous innovation. Nevertheless, the cost advantages realized in the licensing, construction, and operation processes may well outweigh this drawback. Moreover, innovation can still occur under the proviso that improvements are applied to all plants of the same design.

Nuclear Waste. Spent nuclear fuel is currently being stored at reactor sites, but as these on-site facilities near capacity, it will be necessary to find a permanent disposal site regardless of whether any new nuclear plants are built in the United States. A scientific consensus has emerged that the best means of permanent disposal is "geologic isolation"— that is, disposal deep beneath the earth's surface. Under the Nuclear Waste Policy Act of 1982, the Department of Energy was assigned the responsibility of finding a suitable place for a geologic repository and for designing, constructing, and operating it. Yucca Mountain in Nevada has been identified as a potentially suitable location for a repository, and after a lengthy delay because of objections by the state of Nevada, work has now commenced on the necessary scientific study of the site. Under a provision of the 1992 Energy Policy Act, the EPA will issue new radiation standards for the site that may be more realistic than existing ones, and ultimately, the Department of Energy hopes to be able to begin receiving spent fuel there by 2010. **CED urges the federal government to fulfill its mandate to identify a sound, safe, permanent repository for nuclear waste while addressing the legitimate concerns of the people of Nevada. If impartial scientific analysis finds Yucca Mountain to be a safe place for a repository, possibilities should be explored for some form of compensation acceptable to the state.**

Although it is to be hoped that problems pertaining to the Yucca Mountain site will ultimately be resolved, it is not certain that the repository will be ready on time, if at all. The industry should therefore speed plans for temporary above-ground storage capacity to meet storage needs until the issue of a permanent repository is settled.

Conclusion. Recent legislation on nuclear plant licensing, industry initiatives to make nuclear power cost-effective and safe, and the promise of more advanced reactor designs lead us to the conclusion that the nuclear industry need not be bound by its past mistakes and disappointing economic performance. An efficient nuclear industry could provide significant social benefits. However, a stable regulatory environment and continued industry commitment to the agenda it has set for itself will be required if nuclear power is to realize its full promise.

RENEWABLE ENERGY

We have argued that the true cost-effectiveness of using a particular energy source should depend on both the private and social costs of its production and consumption. Analyzing nuclear energy in this light yielded a dual rationale for retaining the nuclear option: (1) the potential for lowering private production costs and (2) the favorable effects on air quality.

A similar rationale exists for the development of renewable energy sources, which include heat and light from the sun, flowing and falling water, wind, organic nonfossil materials, and heat from the earth's crust. Many of these energy forms are environmentally benign compared with fossil fuels. Moreover, some renewable energy sources are cost-effective at least at favorable locations. But their widespread use has been impeded either because they are more expensive than conventional fuels or because their availability is limited in many parts of the country. Cost-effectiveness on a larger scale would be facilitated by improvements in the efficiency of technologies for identifying, extracting, and converting these resources to usable energy forms. Some believe that an aggressive R&D program would overcome many technological hurdles and create the potential for sharply lower production costs.

BENEFITS OF RENEWABLE ENERGY

The potential benefits of renewable energy are well documented. Like nuclear energy, renewable energy sources carry an array of external costs and benefits over the entire fuel cycle. For example, some hydropower projects may have an adverse impact on aquatic life, wetlands, and farmland. Others may provide flood control, community water supplies, and scenic recreational possibilities. The atmospheric effects of using renewable energy sources are usually favorable compared with those of fossil fuels because emissions of CO_2 and other pollutants are minimal or nonexistent in many cases. Biomass and ethanol are possible exceptions. Combustion of biomass releases CO_2, but if the harvested crops or trees are replanted, an equal amount of CO_2 would be reabsorbed during the growth cycle. Whether or not emission and reabsorption of CO_2 net out to zero over time therefore depends upon how biomass resources are managed. However, there are other factors to consider, such as the impact of energy used by farming equipment. The use of ethanol in gasoline —"gasohol"— has an uncertain effect on ozone formation; CO emissions are reduced, but VOC emissions increase because of greater fuel volatility.

Domestically produced renewable energy displaces imported energy sources and exerts downward pressure on the prices of all fuels. The added diversification that greater use of renewable energy could contribute to the U.S. energy portfolio would help to even out price fluctuations and reduce the risk associated with interruptions to the supply of one major energy source.

Further development of renewable energy technologies (RETs) should create new industries as well as technological spin-offs to other industries and regions.[116] For example, advances in composite materials to improve the efficiency of wind turbine blades may have applications in the auto and aircraft industries, and developments in hard-rock drilling technology to retrieve geothermal resources could benefit the oil and gas industries.[117]

CONSTRAINTS ON DEPLOYMENT

RETs are currently subject to a number of technical and regulatory constraints that frequently make them too costly or inefficient to be used on a large scale. Because capital markets perceive higher risks in renewable energy projects, investments in such projects must offer a higher rate of return.

Exploration and Access to Resources. Techniques for finding various renewable energy sources and accurately estimating their potential need to be improved. Geothermal energy provides a good example. The geothermal industry uses oil and gas technology for exploration, drilling, and site characterization; the lack of specialized technology for these functions adds substantially to the cost of developing the resources.

Conversion Efficiency. The conversion efficiency of equipment governs the amount of an energy resource that is converted to usable form. Inadequate conversion efficiency is an obstacle to greater cost-effectiveness for a large number of renewable energy sources. For example, improvements in the technology of photovoltaic cells and wind turbines would reduce the cost of structures and diminish land requirements.

Storage. Renewable energy sources used to generate electricity will frequently be used for peak-load application without storage. However, for base-load utilization of intermittent sources, such as solar thermal electricity, storage becomes a factor. Further research and development in this area is needed.

Other Problems. Other factors constraining cost-effectiveness include lengthy and complicated licensing requirements for new facilities (*e.g.*, onerous environmental requirements for hydroelectric facilities mandated by the Electric Consumer Protection Act of 1986) and limited scale of equipment manufacture because of uncertain markets. Standardization of equipment and expansion of production scale should serve to reduce costs.

R&D FUNDING

RETs are at different stages of maturity and cost-effectiveness, but in most cases, there is room for considerable advancement in efficiency. However, it is important to appreciate the degree to which costs have already fallen for a number of these sources. For example, Pacific Gas and Electric Company was generating electricity from wind and solar thermal sources for $0.08 and $0.10 per kilowatt-hour (kwh) respectively in 1990, compared with $0.52 and $0.75 in 1980.[118] However, federal R&D spending on RETs declined sharply through the 1980s (from $559 million in 1980 to $139 million in 1990), although appropriations have begun to increase again.[119] Many analysts believe that a modest increase in federal support would generate substantial cost reductions. **CED believes that federal sup-**

port for renewable energy R&D should be given a higher priority than it was during the 1980s. The potential for further improvements in the efficiency of RETs and the anticipated social benefits of these technologies indicate that steady federal support is justifiable and desirable.

SOME PROMISING RENEWABLE ENERGY SOURCES

Wind. Wind power is already economically competitive in parts of the United States. The average cost of production has fallen from more than $0.50 per kwh at the beginning of the 1980s to $0.08 in 1992 and as low as $0.05 at particularly favorable sites. The use of wind power has so far been limited mainly to California, but the Department of Energy believes that 16 states have at least equal wind energy potential.[120] According to both Department and industry analysts, competitively priced wind power will be available even at moderately favorable sites within 20 years. A more efficient, variable-speed wind turbine, currently under development with the support of the utility industry, is expected to realize a consistent production cost of $0.05 per kwh, with $0.03 "not out of reach."[121]

Hydroelectricity. Flowing or falling water is used to generate electricity. This source accounts for a little more than 9 percent of U.S. electricity generation, and still undeveloped resources may be about equal to the capacity of existing facilities.[122] Hydroelectric facilities have high initial capital costs and give rise to environmental concerns related to aquatic life and the impact on adjoining lands. However, it is a clean energy source with no air emissions, low operating costs, and recreational potential. Research on improved turbines could enhance efficiency and make installation of additional hydro facilities cost-effective.

Biomass. Biomass energy is the combustion of organic, nonfossil material, such as crops, wood and wood by-products, and solid waste. This source currently accounts for around 3 percent of U.S. primary energy production, mostly process and space heat used by the pulp, paper, and lumber industries,

and space heating and cooking in the residential sector. Nonrecyclable recovered paper used as a fossil fuel substitute is an example of a developing renewable energy application of solid waste. Liquid fuels are also derived from biomass. An annual amount of 1 billion gallons of ethanol, primarily derived from corn fermentation, is blended with gasoline to make gasohol. The net environmental benefits of gasohol are controversial because the presence of ethanol reduces CO emissions but increases VOCs. (In addition, without federal subsidies aimed at supporting the agricultural sector, ethanol would not be cost-competitive. The Office of Technology Assessment estimates that the production cost per gallon of ethanol is somewhere in the range of $0.85 to $1.50, compared with $0.55 per gallon of gasoline at wholesale. The volumetric energy content of ethanol is only two-thirds that of gasoline.)

The total biomass resource base is potentially very large. However, its volumetric energy content is relatively low, and it will be necessary to develop more productive crops and to utilize more land and water resources. Developments in biotechnology will assist in the former, but there are obvious environmental and land-use implications associated with the latter.

Geothermal. Heat, hot water, or steam taken from beneath the earth's surface are sources of geothermal energy. The resource base both in the United States and worldwide is enormous, but the costs of recovery are in many instances too high to make geothermal energy competitive at the moment. There are some notable exceptions, however. California derives 7 percent of its electricity from geothermal sources.[123] To gain more benefits from the geothermal resource base, R&D is required to improve exploration technology, verification of fields, prediction of field performance, and development of equipment that is resistant to high temperatures and corrosion. Environmental benefits include negligible emissions of CO_2 and other pollutants.

Solar Energy. Mirrors and lenses can be used to focus sunlight, which then heats a liquid to generate electricity. Only a minuscule proportion of U.S. electricity is currently produced by this means, at production costs in the area of $0.12 to $0.15 per kwh.[124] Several technologies in the R&D phase offer some promise of reducing costs in the longer term.

Solar energy is also harnessed directly by solar collectors to provide hot water and space heat in residential and commercial buildings and to provide steam to power machinery. In some instances solar energy has been cost-effective, particularly where it has received favorable tax treatment.

Photovoltaics. Thin semiconductor layers absorb sunlight and convert it directly into electric current. Although costs continue to fall, photovoltaic power still costs $0.20 to $0.30 per kwh and is therefore not currently competitive with conventionally generated electricity. However, advances in semiconductors and microelectronics should increase the effi-ciency of photovoltaic devices and lower costs to a competitive level within the next 20 years.[125]

Municipal Solid Waste. Solid waste from households and businesses can be burned for process heat or to produce steam and then electricity. However, capital and operating costs are relatively high, and the combustion process causes both air emissions and solid residues.

Ocean Technologies. Ocean thermal energy conversion, which exploits temperature differences between surface and deep water, and other technologies that use wave and tidal power face significant technical barriers and are not yet commercialized to any extent in the United States. There are few promising locations in this country for future application of these technologies.

APPENDIX TABLE

NATIONAL AMBIENT AIR QUALITY STANDARDS (NAAQS) IN EFFECT IN 1992

POLLUTANT	PRIMARY (HEALTH RELATED)		SECONDARY (WELFARE RELATED)	
	Type of Average	Standard Level Concentration[a]	Type of Average	Standard Level Concentration
CO	8-hour[b]	9 ppm (10 mg/m³)	No Secondary Standard	
	1-hour[b]	35ppm (40 mg/m³)	No Secondary Standard	
Pb	Maximum Quarterly Average	1.5 µg/m³	Same as Primary Standard	
NO₂	Annual Arithmetic Mean	0.053 ppm (100 µg/m³)	Same as Primary Standard	
O₃	Maximum Daily 1-hour Average[c]	0.12 ppm (235 µg/m³)	Same as Primary Standard	
PM-10	Annual Arithmetic Mean[d]	50 µg/m³	Same as Primary Standard	
	24-hour[d]	150 µg/m³	Same as Primary Standard	
SO₂	Annual Arithmetic Mean	80 µg/m³ (0.03 ppm)	3-hour[b]	1300 µg/m³ (0.50 ppm)
	24-hour[b]	365 µg/m³ (0.14 ppm)		

(a) Parenthetical value is an approximately equivalent concentration.

(b) Not to be exceeded more than once per year.

(c) The standard is attained when the expected number of days per calendar year with maximum hourly average concentrations above 0.12 ppm is equal to or less than 1, as determined according to Appendix H of the Ozone NAAQS.

(d) Particulate standards use PM-10 (particles less than 10µ in diameter) as the indicator pollutant. The annual standard is attained when the expected annual arithmetic mean concentration is less than or equal to 50 µg/m³; the 24-hour standard is attained when the expected number of days per calendar year above 150 µg/m³ is equal to or less than 1; as determined according to Appendix K of the PM NAAQS.

SOURCE: Reproduced from Environmental Protection Agency, *National Air Quality and Emissions Trends Report, 1991*, p. 2-1.

NOTES

CHAPTER 1

1. For a recent review of studies on this issue, see Maureen L. Cropper and Wallace E. Oates, "Environmental Economics: A Survey," *Journal of Economic Literature* 30 (June 1992): 685-692.

2. It can be demonstrated that compliance costs are minimized when the incremental cost of compliance is equalized across all emission sources. Market-based incentives encourage each firm to reduce emissions until the incremental cost just equals the emission charge (or permit value) and thereby automatically equalize incremental compliance costs. Regulators do not have sufficient information on the costs of individual polluters to achieve this least-cost outcome even if this is their intent.

3. This refers to regions that do not meet federal standards for ambient air quality.

4. National Research Council, *Automotive Fuel Economy: How Far Should We Go?* (Washington, DC: National Academy Press, 1992), p. 7.

5. CED has encouraged the U.S. government to "push the issue of family planning onto the international agenda" not only to relieve pressures on the environment but also to encourage economic growth. Committee for Economic Development, *The United States in the New Global Economy: A Rallier of Nations* (New York, NY: CED, 1992), pp. 55-59.

6. Forests are one of the four natural "sinks" which absorb CO_2. In addition, the process of deforestation often releases large quantities of CO_2.

7. Committee for Economic Development, *Restoring Prosperity: Budget Choices for Economic Growth* (New York, NY: CED, 1992), p. 8.

8. The EPA estimates that by the year 2000, highway vehicle use will account for 12 percent of hydrocarbon emissions, down from about 24 percent in 1990. U.S. Environmental Protection Agency, *National Air Pollutant Emission Estimates 1900-1991* (Research Triangle Park, NC: U.S. EPA, October 1992), p. 74.

9. Gross petroleum imports are reported to have risen to 46.2 percent of domestic consumption in 1992. "Domestic Energy Concerns Favor Fee on Oil Imports Over Gasoline Tax Rise," *The Wall Street Journal* (January 15, 1993): A2. The dependence issue has been a concern of the United States since the 1973 Arab oil embargo. A 1974 CED statement addressed this issue. Committee for Economic Development, *Achieving Energy Independence* (New York, NY: CED, 1974), p. 13. It was also discussed in Thomas C. Schelling, *Thinking Through the Energy Problem*, CED Supplementary Paper (New York, NY: CED, 1979), p. 32.

10. These include "no regrets" policies advocated by the Bush Administration.

CHAPTER 2

1. The British Petroleum Company plc, *BP Statistical Review of World Energy* (London, United Kingdom: BP, June 1991), p. 35. U.S. Department of Energy, Energy Information Administration, *International Energy Outlook 1992* (Washington, DC: U.S. Government Printing Office, April 1992), p. 27.

2. For example, while OECD consumption increased by 14 percent between 1981 and 1991, consumption by the six members of the Association of Southeast Asian Nations went up by 94 percent. See British Petroleum Company plc, *BP Statistical Review of World Energy* (London, United Kingdom: BP, June 1992), p. 33.

3. British Petroleum, *BP Statistical Review of World Energy* (June 1992), p. 29.

4. U.S. Department of Energy, *International Energy Outlook 1992*, p. 27.

5. From a longer perspective, it appears that there has been a secular improvement in energy efficiency since World War I. This trend temporarily stalled during the 20-year period to 1973. See S. H. Schurr, "Energy Use, Technological Change, and Productive Efficiency: An Economic-Historical Interpretation," *Annual Review of Energy 1984*, 9 (1984): 412.

6. See U.S. Department of Energy, Energy Information Administration, *Indicators of Energy Efficiency: An International Comparison* (Washington, DC: U.S. Government Printing Office, July 1990), pp. 6-7.

7. One study put the improvement in manufacturing energy efficiency at 2.5 percent a year between 1958 and 1973 and only fractionally higher—2.7 percent—from 1973 to 1985. See Lee Schipper, Richard B. Howarth, and Howard Geller, "United States Energy Use From 1973 to 1987: The Impacts of Improved Efficiency" in *Annual Review of Energy 1990*, 15 (1990): 455-504.

8. S. H. Schurr, "Energy Use, Technological Change, and Productive Efficiency: An Economic-Historical Interpretation," and Mark P. Mills, *Ecowatts: The Clean Switch — Using Electricity to Save Energy and Cut Greenhouse Gases* (Chevy Chase, MD: Science Concepts, Inc., April 1991). See also Chauncey Starr, "Implications of Continuing Electrification," p. 54, and Alvin M. Weinberg, "Energy in Retrospect: Is the Past Prologue?" p. 26, both in National Academy of Engineering, *Energy: Production, Consumption, and Consequences* (Washington, DC: National Academy Press, 1990).

9. Weinberg, "Energy in Retrospect: Is the Past Prologue?" p. 26.

10. Studies have estimated the separate effects of structural changes and energy efficiency on energy intensity. See Schipper, Howarth, and Geller, "United States Energy Use From 1973 to 1987: The Impacts of Improved Efficiency," and John Preston, Robert Adler, and Mark Schipper, "Energy Efficiency in the Manufacturing Sector," U.S. Department of Energy, Energy Information Administration, *Monthly Energy Review, December 1992* (Washington, DC: U.S. Government Printing Office, December 1992), pp. 1-7.

11. Important developments behind this improvement were an *increase* of more than one-third in power per unit of engine size (displacement) and a reduction in the ratio of car weight to interior volume. Marc Ross, "Energy and Transportation," *Annual Review of Energy 1989*, 14 (1989):145. The contribution of CAFE and rising energy prices are discussed in Chapter 4.

12. The projection shown in Figure 14 is the Energy Information Administration's reference case, which assumes that the economy will grow at an annual rate of 2.0 percent and that the

price of oil will hover between $19 and $23 per barrel until the end of the decade, rising to $29 per barrel (in 1991 dollars) by 2010. For alternate scenarios, see U.S. Department of Energy, Energy Information Administration, *Annual Energy Outlook 1993 with Projections to 2010* (Washington, DC: U.S. Government Printing Office, January 1993), p. 3.

13. In 1991, U.S. coal exports were 11 percent of production.

14. The Department of Energy estimates that productivity of surface mines in 1990 was 6.1 tons per miner hour, compared with 2.5 tons in underground mines. See U.S. Department of Energy, Energy Information Administration, *Annual Energy Review 1991* (Washington, DC: U.S. Government Printing Office, June 1992), p. 185.

15. For a comparison of forecasts, see U.S. Department of Energy, Energy Information Administration, *Annual Energy Outlook 1993 with Projections to 2010*, p. 74. Forecasts range from 47 percent dependency (Gas Research Institute) to 61 percent (DRI/McGraw-Hill).

16. The ratio of proved reserves to production is defined here as the reserves at the end of any one year divided by production in that same year. The data are drawn from British Petroleum, *BP Statistical Review of World Energy* (June 1992), p. 2.

17. For example, the 1978 Fuel Use Act prohibited gas use in baseload power generation.

18. The world R/P ratio stood at 59 years at the end of 1991. See British Petroleum, *BP Statistical Review of World Energy* (June 1992), p. 18.

19. U.S. Department of Energy, Energy Information Administration, *Commercial Nuclear Power 1991: Prospects for the United States and the World* (Washington, DC: U.S. Government Printing Office, August 1991), p. 34.

20. For estimates of the costs of renewable energy sources, see Chapter 4.

21. An interlaboratory white paper prepared for the Administration's National Energy Strategy in March 1990 claims that with currently projected prices, an intensified federally assisted research and development effort could advance the contribution of renewable energy (including methanol and ethanol) to 28 percent of total domestic energy needs by 2030. The labs predicted that this goal could be achieved with an additional $3 billion in federal funding over the next 20 years. It should be kept in mind, however, that the labs would be direct beneficiaries of such a program. See Solar Energy Research Institute, *The Potential of Renewable Energy: An Interlaboratory White Paper* (Golden, CO: Solar Energy Research Institute, March 1990).

22. See, for example, Congress of the United States, Office of Technology Assessment, *Replacing Gasoline: Alternative Fuels for Light-Duty Vehicles* (Washington, DC: U.S. Government Printing Office, 1990).

23. For information on developing countries, see United Nations Environment Programme and World Health Organization, *Assessment of Urban Air Quality* (Nairobi, Kenya: UNEP, 1989).

24. Most frequently, health problems are insidious, resulting from prolonged exposure to pollutants. But on at least two occasions, once in Britain and once in the United States, large numbers of people were killed by pollution. The first of these was in Donora, Pennsylvania in 1948, but the 1952 acute episode of "black fog" in London, which is widely reported to have claimed 4,000 lives, is apparently the most severe case on record.

25. In addition to these primary standards for health, secondary standards were established for nonhealth reasons. A summary of the primary EPA standards is shown in the Appendix Table (page 83). For a summary of these standards and their measurement, see U.S. Environmental Protection Agency, Office of Air Quality Planning and Standards, *National Air Quality and Emissions Trends Report, 1991* (Research Triangle Park, NC: U.S. EPA, October 1992). Particulate matter was previously designated total suspended particulate (TSP). The ozone referred to here is ground-level ozone, not stratospheric ozone.

26. Paul R. Portney, "Air Pollution Policy," *Public Policies for Environmental Protection*, ed. Paul R. Portney (Washington, DC: Resources for the Future, 1990), pp. 31-33.

27. Executive Office of the President, Council on Environmental Quality, co-sponsored by the Interagency Advisory Committee on Environmental Trends, *Environmental Trends, 1989* (Washington, DC: U.S. Government Printing Office, 1989), pp. 63-69.

28. The effect of federal regulation on air quality is controversial because it is difficult to separate the independent effects of regulations, changes in energy prices, and consumption of energy resulting from fluctuations in economic activity. Some studies have suggested that state regulations promulgated prior to federal involvement had larger effects. See, for example, Robert W. Crandall, *Controlling Industrial Pollution: The Economics and Politics of Clean Air* (Washington, DC: The Brookings Institution, 1983), p. 19.

29. Hilary French, "Clearing the Air," *State of the World*, ed. Lester Brown *et al.* (New York, NY: W. W. Norton & Co., 1990), pp. 98-110.

30. U.S. Environmental Protection Agency, *National Air Quality and Emissions Trends Report, 1991.*

31. A recent study suggests that VOC emissions in urban areas may be underestimated.

32. VOC emissions from highway vehicles decreased 11 percent between 1990 and 1991, according to the EPA, reflecting the ongoing Federal Motor Vehicle Control Program (FMVCP) and new measures to lower Reid vapor pressure (Rvp) in gasoline. U.S. Environmental Protection Agency, *National Air Pollutant Emission Estimates 1900-1991* (Research Triangle Park, NC: U.S. EPA, October 1992), p. 108.

33. U.S. Environmental Protection Agency, *National Air Quality and Emissions Trends Report, 1991*, pp. 1-6.

34. R.L. Polk & Co., cited in Motor Vehicle Manufacturers Association, *MVMA Motor Vehicle Facts & Figures '91* (Detroit, MI: MVMA, 1991).

35. According to the EPA, half of all power plant emissions are produced by 50 industrial plants in 15 states. See U.S. Environmental Protection Agency, *National Air Quality and Emissions Trends Report, 1989* (Research Triangle Park, NC: U.S. EPA, February 1991), pp. 1-5.

36. We have not included the separate issue of toxic air pollutants in this description because this policy statement focuses primarily on air quality problems arising solely from energy consumption. The 1970 Amendments to the Clean Air Act did not successfully control the emission of many hazardous pollut-

ants. In some instances, state programs have filled the void, but the result has been a patchwork of overlapping regulations. Approximately 1.3 million tons of toxic air pollutants are released each year in the United States, primarily by chemical and manufacturing facilities. Energy-related sources of toxics include oil- and coal-fueled boilers, petroleum refineries, oil and gas exploration and production, and waste-to-energy plants. In addition, benzene and diesel particulate emissions from motor vehicles may present a significant risk. See U.S. Department of Energy, *National Energy Strategy* (Washington, DC: U.S. Government Printing Office, February 1991), p. 165. The 1990 Amendments to the Clean Air Act set up a new program to control 189 pollutants.

37. U.S. Environmental Protection Agency, *National Air Quality and Emissions Trends Report, 1991*, pp. 6, 8, and 14.

38. The areas designated as nonattainment that met NAAQS in the 1989-91 period are not automatically redesignated as attainment. Attainment status depends on meeting two further conditions: An area must have (1) an approved State Implementation Plan (SIP) and (2) "an approved maintenance plan showing attainment for ten years." U.S. Environmental Protection Agency, "Air Trends Fact Sheet," released October 19, 1992.

39. National Research Council, *Rethinking the Ozone Problem in Urban and Regional Air Pollution* (Washington, DC: National Academy Press, 1991), pp. 4-16.

40. U.S. Environmental Protection Agency, *National Air Quality and Emissions Trends Report, 1991*, pp. 5-1 to 5-7. The PSI "integrates information from many pollutants across the entire monitoring network into a single number which represents the worst daily air quality experienced in the urban area."

41. Executive Office of the President, Council on Environmental Quality, co-sponsored by the Interagency Advisory Committee on Environmental Trends, *Environmental Trends, 1989*, pp. 68-69.

42. U.S. National Acid Precipitation Assessment Program, *Acid Deposition: State of Science and Technology, Summary Report* (Washington, DC: NAPAP, September 1991).

43. Intergovernmental Panel on Climate Change, *Policy Makers' Summary of the Scientific Assessment of Climate Change* (Bracknell, United Kingdom: IPCC Group, Meteorological Office, 1990).

44. Intergovernmental Panel on Climate Change, *IPCC 1992 Supplement Science Assessment* (Bracknell, United Kingdom: IPCC Group, Meteorological Office, 1990).

45. National Academy of Sciences, *Policy Implications of Greenhouse Warming*, (Washington, DC: National Academy Press, 1991), p. 10. CO_2 emitted into the atmosphere moves among four "sinks": the atmosphere, the oceans, the soil, and the earth's biomass. However, in the current accounting of the disposition of CO_2 emissions, 45 percent of emissions from human activity are missing. The Academy study recommended using 40 percent of emissions as the atmospheric accumulation rate of CO_2, (p. 88).

46. Congress of the United States, Office of Technology Assessment, *Changing by Degrees: Steps to Reduce Greenhouse Gases* (Washington, D.C.: U.S. Government Printing Office, February 1991). Chapter 2 contains summary descriptions of GHGs and the ozone depletion issue.

47. For a recent evaluation of these findings, see William R. Cline, *The Economics of Global Warming* (Washington, DC: Institute for International Economics, 1992), pp. 17-19 and 59-61.

48. This is the revised IPCC estimate. The National Academy study showed a range of 1.9 to 5.2 degrees centigrade. National Academy of Sciences, *Policy Implications of Greenhouse Warming*, p. 2. The Academy states that the numerical computer simulations using general circulation models (or GCMs) "are generally considered the best available tools for anticipating climate changes," (p. 17).

49. Intergovernmental Panel on Climate Change, *Policy Makers' Summary of the Scientific Assessment of Climate Change* and *IPCC 1992 Supplement Science Assessment*.

50. For a summary of the views of critics, see A. Fred Singer, *Global Warming: Do We Know Enough to Act?* (St. Louis, MO: Center for the Study of American Business, Washington University, March 1991), pp. 4-12.

51. William Nordhaus, "Global Warming: Slowing the Greenhouse Express," *Setting National Priorities*, ed. Henry Aaron (Washington, DC: The Brookings Institution, 1990), pp. 192-209.

52. International Energy Agency, *Greenhouse Gas Emissions: The Energy Dimension* (Paris, France: OECD/IEA, April 1991). While total CO_2 emissions are projected to rise, the OECD member countries' contribution to CO_2 emissions is projected to decline from 45 percent in 1987 to 37 percent in 2005, (pp. 44-45).

53. Estimates of emissions of CO_2 (in metric tons) per $1,000 in GNP for China, India, and Mexico are 6.01, 2.52, and 1.74, respectively. For the United States, the figure is 0.98. National Academy of Sciences, *Policy Implications of Greenhouse Warming*, p. 8.

CHAPTER 3

1. U.S. Environmental Protection Agency, *Environmental Investments: The Cost of a Clean Environment* (Washington, DC: U.S. EPA, 1990). These figures do not include significant indirect costs encountered by many firms, such as a shift to higher-cost inputs in order to comply with a regulation. Council of Economic Advisers, *Economic Report of the President* (Washington, DC: U.S. Government Printing Office, February 1992), p. 183.

2. Dale W. Jorgenson and Peter J. Wilcoxen, "Environmental Regulation and U.S. Economic Growth," *Rand Journal of Economics* (Summer 1990): 314-340.

3. Michael Hazilla and Raymond J. Kopp, "Social Cost of Environmental Quality Regulation: A General Equilibrium Analysis," *Journal of Political Economy* 98, no. 4 (August 1990): 853-873.

4. The political difficulty of enacting environmental legislation that requires least-cost regulatory methods has led some experts to call for more research on ways to design efficient regulation subject to practical political constraints. See Robert W. Hahn and Roger G. Noll, *Environmental Markets in the Year 2000* (Stanford, CA: Center for Economic Policy Research, Stanford University, 1990).

5. Paul R. Portney, ed., *Public Policies for Environmental Protection* (Washington, DC: Resources for the Future, 1990), p. 13. Prior to

this century, all air pollution problems were handled under the nuisance and trespass provisions of common laws, according to Portney. Strong incentives to reduce pollution could be provided by the legal system only if property rights to clean air were clearly defined and polluters could be held liable for damage.

6. Portney, *Public Policies for Environmental Protection*, p. 32.

7. For a brief discussion of technology-based standards, see T.H. Tietenberg, *Environmental and Natural Resource Economics*, 3d ed. (New York, NY: Harper-Collins Publishers, 1992), p. 396.

8. The costs of this program relative to health benefits may turn out to be extremely high. It has been estimated that the 1 million annual new cancer cases might be reduced by 500 at a cost as high as $6 to $10 billion. See Robert Crandall, *Why Is the Cost of Environmental Regulation So High?* (St. Louis, MO: Center for the Study of American Business, Washington University, February 1992), p. 12.

9. Tietenberg, *Environmental and Natural Resource Economics*, p. 394. The Clean Air Act did not specifically forbid consideration of costs. However, the zero-risk standard suggests that costs and feasibility cannot be taken into account; and on several occasions, the courts have ruled that costs may not be considered in setting ambient air standards. Indeed, the courts have ruled that the Clean Air Act "speaks only of protecting public health and welfare" and that "the statute and its legislative history make clear that economic considerations play no part in the promulgation of ambient air quality standards. . . ." See "Lead Industries Association, Inc. vs. Environmental Protection Agency," *Environmental Law Reporter* (August 1980): 10 ELR 20651.

10. According to Portney, rather than admitting that a stricter standard is not worth pursuing in view of its cost, the decision not to adopt such a standard has usually been justified by pointing out uncertainty about the added health protection that would be afforded by a stricter standard. See Portney, *Public Policies for Environmental Protection*, p. 77.

11. For a recent presentation of benefit-cost principles and economic efficiency, see Edward M. Gramlich, *A Guide to Benefit-Cost Analysis* (Englewood Cliffs, NJ: Prentice-Hall, 1990).

12. National Research Council, P. Brett Hammond and Rob Coppoch, eds., *Valuing Health Risks, Costs and Benefits for Environmental Decision Making* (Washington, DC: National Academy Press, 1990). For a recent survey of techniques used in the monetary valuation of health and morbidity benefits, see OECD, *Environmental Policy Benefits: Monetary Valuation* (Paris, France: OECD, 1989).

13. Such a change in policy would require enactment of legislation.

14. Benefit-cost analysis may not be an appropriate tool for analyzing all environmental issues. Some scholars argue that it should not be applied to issues involving basic societal values. For example, some believe that it is not appropriate to quantify the "existence value" of wilderness areas, in part because this issue pertains to relationships between humans and nature. For a recent discussion on this issue, see Donald Rosenthal and Robert Nelson, "Why Existence Value Should Not Be Used in Cost-Benefit Analysis," *Journal of Policy Analysis and Management,* no. 1 (Winter 1992): 116-122.

15. Indeed, in the unlikely circumstance that the cost of abatement is the same in urban and rural areas, a mandatory uniform standard that requires equal abatement expenditures in both areas would imply that regulators place a much higher value on the health of individuals living in rural areas than on those in urban areas.

16. See Leonard Gianessi, Henry Peskin, and Edward Wolff, "The Distributional Effects of Uniform Air Pollution Policy in the United States," *The Quarterly Journal of Economics* (May 1979): 281-301. The authors found just four places in the country (all in the New York City-northeastern New Jersey area) with net benefits from uniform automobile emission standards. Of 274 areas studied, only 61 showed net benefits from industrial pollution control policy. Putting the industry and automobile policies together, only 28 percent of the entire U.S. population enjoyed positive net benefits.

17. See, for example, Michael T. Maloney and Gordon L. Brady, "Capital Turnover and Marketable Pollution Rights," *Journal of Law and Economics* (April 1988): 203-226.

18. A $3 billion reduction in control costs from $7 to $4 billion has been cited. See Crandall, *Why Is the Cost of Environmental Regulation So High?* p. 10.

19. The principle that total compliance costs are minimized when incremental compliance costs are equalized across emission sources is well established. See, for example, Tietenberg, *Environmental and Natural Resource Economics,* pp. 369-370.

20. Michael H. Levin, "Statutes and Stopping Points: Building a Better Bubble at EPA," *Regulation* (March-April 1985): 39. Also see Maloney and Brady, "Capital Turnover and Marketable Pollution Rights," and Congress of the United States, Congressional Budget Office, *Environmental Regulation and Economic Efficiency* (Washington, DC: CBO, 1985), p. 9.

21. See T. H. Tietenberg, *Emissions Trading: An Exercise in Reforming Pollution Policy* (Washington, DC: Resources for the Future, 1985), pp. 42-43. The additional administrative costs engendered by flexible market-based approaches to pollution control are low relative to the benefits.

22. See Portney, *Public Policies for Environmental Protection,* pp. 76-77.

23. The principal mandate for NO_x under Title IV is that 111 coal-fired utilities become subject to new emissions standards beginning January 1, 1995. The EPA is also required to submit a report to Congress on January 1, 1994, on the environmental and economic consequences of emissions trading between SO_2 and NO_x.

24. See Portney, *Public Policies for Environmental Protection,* p. 77.

25. See International Energy Agency, *Energy and the Environment: Policy Overview* (Paris, France: IEA/OECD, 1989), p. 70.

26. See Congress of the United States, Congressional Budget Office, "Environmental Federalism: Allocating Responsibilities for Environmental Protection," (Staff Working Paper, September 1988), especially Chapter 2.

27. See Crandall, *Why Is the Cost of Environmental Regulation So High?* pp. 18-19.

1. George C. Marshall Institute, *Global Warming Update: Recent Scientific Findings* (Washington, DC: George C. Marshall Institute, 1992), p. 10.

2. National Academy of Sciences, *Policy Implications of Greenhouse Warming,* (Washington, DC: National Academy Press, 1991), pp. 80-81.

3. National Academy of Sciences, *Policy Implications of Greenhouse Warming,* p. 98.

4. Higher temperatures are expected to increase atmospheric concentrations of water vapor, the most important GHG. However, the effects of changing moisture on cloud formation and reflectivity of incoming sunlight are not certain. It is not known whether the net effect of this and other such feedback effects will be to raise temperatures further.

5. National Academy of Sciences, *Policy Implications of Greenhouse Warming,* pp. 24 and 102.

6. A counsel to the President described "no regrets" as "a policy of adopting those environmental measures that reduce greenhouse gas emissions while providing concrete environmental benefits." C. Boyden Gray and David B. Renkin, Jr., "A 'No Regrets' Environmental Policy," *Foreign Policy* 83 (Summer 1991): 52.

7. Council of Economic Advisers, *Economic Report of the President* (Washington, DC: U.S. Government Printing Office, 1990), pp. 223-224.

8. World Bank, *World Development Report 1992: Development and the Environment* (New York, NY: Oxford University Press, 1992), p. 11.

9. International Energy Agency, *The Role of IEA Governments in Energy* (Paris, France: OECD/IEA, 1992), pp. 23-25.

10. World Bank, *World Development Report 1992: Development and the Environment,* p. 12.

11. William R. Cline, *Global Warming: The Economic Stakes* (Washington, DC: Institute for International Economics, 1992), p. 66.

12. World Bank, *World Development Report 1992: Development and the Environment,* p. 163.

13. It is usually proposed that a carbon tax be levied at the import or production stage and that a rebate be paid for processing that reduces the fuel's carbon content or for use of the product for purposes other than as a fuel.

14. For a discussion of the merits of carbon taxes and tradable permits, see Michael A. Toman and Stephen M. Gardiner, *The Limits of Economic Instruments for International Greenhouse Gas Control* (Washington, DC: Resources for the Future, December 1991). See also Roger C. Dower and Mary Beth Zimmerman, *The Right Climate for Carbon Taxes: Creating Economic Incentives to Protect the Atmosphere* (Washington, DC: World Resources Institute, 1992).

15. Congress of the United States, Congressional Budget Office, *Carbon Charges as a Response to Global Warming: The Effects of Taxing Fossil Fuels* (Washington, DC: U.S. Government Printing Office, August 1990), pp. 25-26.

16. In fact, spokesmen for some developing countries have indicated that they view the global climate change issue as an opportunity to place demands on advanced nations.

17. Wallace E. Oates, *Pollution Charges as a Source of Public Revenues,* Discussion Paper QE92-05 (Washington, DC: Resources for the Future, 1991), p. 5.

18. Congress of the United States, Congressional Budget Office, *Reducing the Deficit: Spending and Revenue Options* (Washington, DC: CBO, 1993), p. 404.

19. William R. Cline, *The Economics of Global Warming* (Washington, DC: Institute for International Economics, June 1992), pp. 185-190.

20. See comments by Paul Joskow following the article by Dale W. Jorgenson, Daniel T. Slesnick, and Peter J. Wilcoxen, "Carbon Taxes and Economic Welfare," *Brookings Papers on Economic Activity, Microeconomics 1992,* eds. Martin Neil Baily and Clifford Winston (Washington, DC: The Brookings Institution, 1992), pp. 432-443.

21. William D. Nordhaus, "To Slow or Not to Slow: The Economics of the Greenhouse Effect," *The Economic Journal* 101 (1991): 920-937.

22. William R. Cline, *Global Warming: The Economic Stakes.*

23. Because the costs are incurred many years before any benefits are derived, benefits and costs cannot be compared unless they are converted to present value terms. As explained in Chapter 3 box "Benefit-Cost Analysis and Environmental Standards," the choice of discount rates is critical and controversial in benefit-cost evaluations. High discount rates sharply decrease estimates of the present value of future benefits and thereby decrease the benefit-cost ratio. It is generally agreed that the appropriate rate is the opportunity cost of capital, but it is not easy to determine this rate for the public sector. For a detailed discussion of this issue, see Edward M. Gramlich, *A Guide To Benefit-Cost Analysis* (Englewood Cliffs, NJ: Prentice-Hall, 1990), pp. 92-114.

24. Nordhaus, "To Slow or Not to Slow: The Economics of the Greenhouse Effect," pp. 930-931.

25. In a more recent study, Nordhaus has attempted to estimate global benefits and costs for alternative emission reduction policies. He estimates that the most efficient policy would be a 10 percent reduction in emissions from a no control baseline. "An Optimal Transaction Path for Controlling Greenhouse Gases," *Science* 258 (November 20, 1992): 1315-1319.

26. The term "combined-cycle" refers to the use of both gas- and steam-fired turbines in the one system. The fuel is burned in a combustion turbine to generate electricity. The exhaust gases exiting the combustion turbine are then used to convert water into steam and generate more electricity. SO_2 emissions are essentially zero, being dependent on natural gas sulphur content; NO_x emissions can be less than 10ppm at 15 percent O_2 in the exhaust, CO emissions are less than 10 ppm, and CO_2 emissions are about 40 percent those of comparable coal-fired plants.

27. This is illustrated by the persistence of urban ozone despite ever tighter emission controls. Implementation of the 1990 Amendments to the Clean Air Act is expected to reduce emissions of common pollutants even if energy consumption in the United States proceeds on its current trend without any strenu-

ous conservation effort. However, the costs greatly exceed the benefits. See U.S. Environmental Protection Agency, *National Air Pollutant Emission Estimates 1900-1991* (Research Triangle Park, NC: U.S. EPA, October 1992), pp. 67-74. See also Alliance to Save Energy *et al.*, *America's Energy Choices: Investing in a Strong Economy and a Clean Environment* (Cambridge, MA: Union of Concerned Scientists, 1991). In its reference (baseline) case, this study predicts a decline in sulphur dioxide and nitrogen oxides through 2030.

28. U.S. Department of Energy, Energy Information Administration, *Energy Consumption and Conservation Potential: Supporting Analysis for the National Energy Strategy* (Washington, DC: U.S. Department of Energy, 1990), p. 3.

29. Electric Power Research Institute, *Efficient Electricity Use: Estimates of Maximum Energy Savings* (Washington, DC: EPRI, March 1990).

30. See Amory B. Lovins and L. Hunter Lovins, "Least-Cost Climatic Stabilization," *Annual Review of Energy* 16 (1991): 433-531. See also A. Fickett, C. Gellings, and A. Lovins, "Efficient Use of Electricity," *Scientific American* (September 1990): 65-74.

31. For a concise discussion of the options, see Jose Goldemberg *et al.*, *Energy for a Sustainable World* (New Delhi, India: Wiley Eastern Limited, 1988), pp. 106-107.

32. In a typical utility conservation program, the utility identifies potential areas for conservation, such as lighting or weatherization, and then encourages implementation of appropriate conservation measures by means of subsidy, information programs, and so on. The costs incurred are then charged back to consumers in the form of higher electricity rates. For examples of some successful utility programs, see Bruce Smart, *Beyond Compliance: A New Industry View of the Environment* (Washington, DC: World Resources Institute, April 1992), pp. 47-52.

33. Paul Joskow and Donald Marron, "What Does a Negawatt Really Cost?" *The Energy Journal* 13, no. 4: 41-74.

34. Joskow and Marron, *What Does a Negawatt Really Cost?*, pp. 62-64.

35. International Energy Agency, *Energy Efficiency and the Environment* (Paris, France: OECD/IEA, 1991), p. 112. The Rocky Mountain Institute claims that just changing the lights from incandescent to fluorescent bulbs would save money even before accounting for the electricity savings because it is not necessary to replace the bulbs as frequently. See Fickett, Gellings, and Lovins, "Efficient Use of Electricity," pp. 66-67.

36. Joskow and Marron, *What Does a Negawatt Really Cost?* Table 3, p. 56.

37. Information supplied by Stephen Anderson, Director of Energy Development, International Paper Company. For other examples of opportunities for improved energy efficiency in the industrial sector, see Manufacturers Alliance for Productivity and Innovation, *Energy Efficiency in the 1990s: An Industry Perspective* (Washington, DC: March 1992).

38. Overall economic efficiency, which demands maximization of benefits from scarce resources, suggests that energy-efficient investments should be on an equal footing with other investments. For a survey of the research, see Kenneth Train, "Dis-

count Rates in Consumers' Energy-Related Decisions: A Review of the Literature," *Energy* 10, no. 12 (1985): 1243-1253.

39. Measuring these externalities associated with energy consumption is a challenge. See Paul Joskow, "Weighing Environmental Externalities: Let's Do It Right," *The Electricity Journal* (May 1992); Stephen Bernow and Donald Marron, *Valuation of Environmental Externalities For Energy Planning and Operations* (Boston, MA: Tellus Institute, 1990); Karen L. Palmer and Alan Krupnick, "Environmental Costing and Electric Utilities' Planning and Investment," *Resources* (Fall 1991); Harold M. Hubbard, "The Real Cost of Energy," *Scientific American* (April 1991).

40. If marginal costs exceed average costs, marginal-cost pricing may raise a separate regulatory issue involving the disposition of added revenues.

41. For example, some consumers do not like the quality of lighting offered by efficient bulbs.

42. Congress of the United States, Office of Technology Assessment, *Industrial Energy Use* (Washington, DC: OTA, 1983), p. 9. See also International Energy Agency, *Energy Efficiency and the Environment*, p. 98.

43. Studies have indicated that there is a decided direct relationship between income and incidence of investment in energy efficiency. It has also been suggested that apart from purchase price, there is the additional factor that low-income individuals tend to have less education and are less able to make the calculations necessary to determine a cost-effective investment. See Kenneth Train, "Discount Rates in Consumers' Energy-Related Decisions: A Review of the Literature," pp. 1251-1252.

44. In its 1983 study comparing policy options for reducing energy consumption in energy-intensive industries, the Office of Technology Assessment found that lower interest rates were the most effective policy. See Congress of the United States, Office of Technology Assessment, *Industrial Energy Use*.

45. Congress of the United States, Office of Technology Assessment, *Energy Efficiency in the Federal Government: Government by Good Example?* (Washington, DC: OTA, 1991), p. 7.

46. Section 305 of the Energy Policy Act requires the federal government to establish energy standards for new federal buildings and for public and assisted housing. The standards must meet or exceed the current industry model codes.

47. NAECA covers refrigerators and freezers, room air conditioners, central air conditioners, water heaters, furnaces, dishwashers, clothes washers, clothes dryers, direct heating equipment, kitchen ranges and ovens, pool heaters, televisions, and fluorescent lamp ballasts. The new legislation extends standards to electric motors, fluorescent lamps, and plumbing products.

48. See Michael Shepard, "How to Improve Energy Efficiency," *Science* (Summer 1991): 88.

49. B. D. Howard and W. R. Prindle, *Better Building Codes for Energy Efficiency* (Washington, DC: Alliance to Save Energy, June 1991).

50. According to the EPA, the program has achieved some useful results in its first year. About 400 companies had signed up, and some have already reported substantial low-cost sav-

ings from lighting upgrades. U.S. Environmental Protection Agency, *Green Lights Program: The First Year* (Washington, DC: U.S. EPA, February 1992).

51. See Eric Hirst, "Individual and Institutional Behavior Related to Energy Efficiency in Building," *Journal of Environmental Systems* 16, no. 1 (1986-1987): 65-66. For a specific empirical example of the benefit of feedback, see Clive Seligman and John Darley, "Feedback as a Means of Decreasing Residential Energy Consumption," *Journal of Applied Psychology* 62, no. 4 (1977): 363

52. These are fluorescent lamp ballasts, refrigerators and freezers, dishwashers, clothes washers, water heaters, room air conditioners, heat pumps, and furnaces.

53. For a study on consumer responses to the FTC program, see Robert F. Dyer, "A Longitudinal Analysis of the Impact of the Appliance Energy Labeling Program, Final Report" (Submitted to Office of Impact Evaluation, Federal Trade Commission, November 1986).

54. For a summary of these results and illustrative case studies, see Howard Geller *et al.*, "The Role of Federal Research and Development in Advancing Energy Efficiency: A $50 Billion Contribution to the U.S. Economy," *Annual Review of Energy 1987*, 12 (1987): 357-95.

55. For a description of energy-efficient mortgage programs, see *A National Program for Energy-Efficient Mortgage and Home Energy Rating Systems: A Blueprint for Action*. Final Report of the National Collaboration on Home Energy Rating Systems and Mortgage Incentives for Energy Efficiency prepared by the National Renewable Energy Laboratory (Washington, DC: March 1992).

56. About 0.03 percent of mortgage loan applicants have taken advantage of energy-efficient mortgages. See Stephen McDonnell, "Adding EEMs to Your Business Plan Toolbox," *Good Cents* (January-February 1992).

57. These are the Federal Housing Administration, the Department of Veterans Affairs, and the Farmers Home Administration, and two secondary-mortgage lenders: the Federal National Mortgage Association (Fannie Mae) and the Federal Home Loan Mortgage Corporation (Freddie Mac). A number of states, cities, and nongovernment organizations also have programs.

58. In 1961, the California legislature passed the first legislation dealing with mobile source emissions, requiring crankcase devices on vehicles sold in the state. The federal government became involved with the 1965 Amendments to the Clean Air Act and the 1970 National Emissions Standards Act, which set standards and a timetable for reduced automobile exhaust emissions. Following the OPEC oil embargo, Congress enacted mandatory automobile fuel efficiency standards.

59. By the early 1970s, evidence began to accumulate showing that the benefits of the mobile source emission program were well below costs. See Eugene P. Sishin, "Automobile Air Pollution Policy," *Current Issues in U.S. Environmental Policy*, ed. Paul R. Portney (Baltimore, MD: Johns Hopkins University Press, 1978), p. 83.

60. By 1982, both hydrocarbon and carbon monoxide tailpipe emissions from new automobiles were reduced by 96 percent and nitrogen oxide by 76 percent per vehicle mile travelled since the precontrol period. In addition, motor vehicle emissions of lead, a serious health hazard, have been nearly eliminated by converting to lead-free gasolines.

61. International Energy Agency, *Energy and the Environment: Policy Overview* (Paris, France: OECD/IEA, 1989), p. 87.

62. U.S. Department of Labor, Bureau of Labor Statistics, *Producer Price Indexes: Data for October*, various years (Washington, D.C.: U.S. Government Printing Office). These annual amounts do not include other costs such as the cost to refiners of switching to unleaded gasoline.

63. U.S. Environmental Protection Agency, *National Air Quality and Emissions Trends Report, 1991* (Research Triangle Park, NC: U.S. EPA, October 1992), p. 1-10.

64. The Office of Technology Assessment estimates that highway vehicles continue to account for 40 to 45 percent of VOCs in nonattainment areas, with Los Angeles at 66 percent. Congress of the United States, Office of Technology Assessment, *Catching Our Breath—Next Steps for Reducing Urban Ozone* (Washington, DC: U.S. Government Printing Office, 1989).

65. National Research Council, *Automotive Fuel Economy: How Far Should We Go?* (Washington, DC: National Academy Press, 1992), p. 3. Safety regulations are expected to add another $300 per vehicle.

66. Robert Crandall, *Why Is the Cost of Environmental Regulation So High?* (St. Louis, MO: Center for the Study of American Business, Washington University, February 1992), p. 11 and p. 23.

67. The proportion of the automobile fleet that is 12 years old or older rose from 11.9 percent in 1980 to 20.8 percent in 1990, and the proportion of light trucks rose from 18.4 to 27.6 percent. Motor Vehicle Manufacturers Association, *MVMA Motor Vehicle Facts & Figures '91* (Detroit, MI: MVMA, 1991), pp. 26-27.

68. Advisory Commission on Intergovernmental Relations, *Automobile Taxes and Fees* (Washington, DC: ACIR, September 1991). These data show that such taxes exist in more than half the states.

69. Robert Anderson, *Reducing Emissions from Older Vehicles*, Report no. 053 (Washington, DC: American Petroleum Institute, August 1990).

70. Gasoline reformulations will involve removal of light volatile hydrocarbons; reduction of sulphur, olefins, aromatics, and benzene; introduction of oxygenators; and diversion of heavier components to diesel and jet fuels.

71. W. J. Hillier and G. L. Ewy, "RFG Will Require Wide Range of Capital Expenditure," *Fuel Reformulation* (January-February 1992): 40-45. An estimate made by Arthur D. Little put the cost to the refining industry at $22 billion with the price of gasoline rising by $0.07 to $0.12 per gallon. See "Gasoline Reformulation Cost Set at $22 Billion," *Journal of Commerce* (August 17, 1991).

72. Turner, Mason and Co., "Northeast Reformulated Gasoline Impacts," DRI/McGraw-Hill for the American Petroleum Institute, *Assessing the Economic Effects of Eastern States Adopting California's Low Emission Vehicle Program*, vol. 2 (Washington, DC: November 1991), Appendix B.

73. National Research Council, *Rethinking the Ozone Problem in Urban and Regional Air Pollution* (Washington, DC: National Academy Press, 1991), p. 13.

74. Alan J. Krupnick, *Vehicle Emissions, Urban Smog and Clean Air Policy* (Washington, DC: Resources for the Future, February 1992), pp. 22-25. Krupnick's calculations indicate that methanol is a very expensive option, costing $33,000 to $60,000 per ton of hydrocarbons reduced.

75. Proposals of this sort have been made for many years. See, for example, Edwin S. Mills and Lawrence V. White, "Government Policies Toward Automated Emissions Control," *Approaches to Control Air Pollution*, ed. Ann F. Friedlander (Cambridge, MA: MIT Press, 1978), pp. 348-402.

76. In most nonattainment areas, ozone levels generally reach unacceptable levels for only a limited number of days per year and for only a few hours on each of those days. In congested areas, the imposition of high pollution fees on those days may be a more cost-effective approach to controlling pollution than added devices on vehicles or reformulated fuels. Crandall, *Why Is the Cost of Environmental Regulation So High?* p. 11.

77. Krupnick, *Vehicle Emissions, Urban Smog and Clean Air Policy*, p. 27.

78. A recent EPA study found that although these autos are driven only 1.7 percent of vehicles miles travelled in the United States, they produce almost 5 percent of national NO_x, 7 percent of national HC, and 7.5 percent of national CO emissions. U.S. Environmental Protection Agency, Office of Mobile Sources, *Accelerated Retirement of Vehicles* (Washington, DC: U.S. EPA, March 1992), p. 1.

79. DRI/McGraw-Hill, *Reducing Energy Consumption by Retiring Older Vehicles: An Alternative to CAFE* (Lexington, MA: DRI/McGraw-Hill, August 1991). The short time frame used in this study (1992 to 1996) may detract from its usefulness because the impact of an accelerated scrappage program will decline relative to increased CAFE as time goes on.

80. For historical data on CAFE standards, see Motor Vehicle Manufacturers Association, *MVMA Motor Vehicle Facts & Figures '91*, p. 74.

81. The President's Council of Economic Advisers concluded in 1986 that the 43 percent increase in average fuel economy between 1973 and 1979 probably should not be attributed to CAFE, given the lag in design and introduction of new models. Council of Economic Advisers, *Economic Report of the President* (Washington, DC: U.S. Government Printing Office, February 1986), p. 177.

82. As a share of that petroleum consumption, net imports of petroleum rose from 36 percent in 1975 to 42 percent in 1990.

83. These factors also inadvertently increase pollution because emissions increase proportionately with miles driven and much more than proportionately with the age of the vehicles.

84. National Research Council, *Automotive Fuel Economy: How Far Should We Go?* p.7.

85. National Research Council, *Automotive Fuel Economy: How Far Should We Go?* p. 4. These costs are in addition to the cost of complying with the Clean Air Act of 1990 ($200 to $1600 per vehicle for Tier I) and new safety regulations ($300 to $500 per passenger vehicle).

86. National Research Council, *Automotive Fuel Economy: How Far Should We Go?* The NRC indicated that the impact on safety is less certain and recommended further research on this issue.

87. National Research Council, *Automotive Fuel Economy: How Far Should We Go?* p. 9.

88. For this reason, it has been proposed that increases in CAFE require "equal effort" from foreign and domestic producers. For example, a bill proposed last year by Senator Richard Bryan (S. 279) would require each firm (domestic and foreign) to achieve equal percentage increases in CAFE from 1988 miles-per-gallon levels. Unlike the original CAFE standard, this approach may put foreign producers at a disadvantage. Domestic manufacturers were hurt most in the area where they were most competitive: the manufacture of large vehicles. According to a former member of President Reagan's Council of Economic Advisers, CAFE permits foreign producers of large luxury vehicles that get low mileage to underprice U.S. manufacturers "not because they are more efficient, but because of CAFE." Thomas Gale Moore, "A Hidden Culprit in Auto Imports," *The Wall Street Journal* (January 14, 1992).

89. The NRC also notes that it is much easier for foreign producers to introduce costly fuel-saving technology required by CAFE than it is for U.S. companies. Foreign manufacturers encounter less resistance to higher prices for fuel-efficient vehicles because foreign consumers more quickly recover this cost due to the high price of gasoline. The NRC regards this as a significant barrier to the export of automobiles produced in the United States by domestic manufacturers. National Research Council, *Automotive Fuel Economy: How Far Should We Go?* p. 103.

90. Committee for Economic Development, *Restoring Prosperity: Budget Choices for Economic Growth* (New York, NY: CED, 1992), p. 8.

91. See Charles River Associates Incorporated, *Policy Alternatives for Reducing Petroleum Use and Greenhouse Emissions* (Boston, MA: CRA, September 1991).

92. W. Kip Viscusi, *Pricing Environmental Risks* (St. Louis, MO: Center for the Study of American Business, Washington University, 1992), pp. 17-20. (Also see box "Economic Consequences of Gasoline Taxes.")

93. As we noted earlier, however, there is some evidence that existing taxes on gasoline are sufficient to internalize the cost to society of local pollution resulting from gasoline consumption.

94. The Energy Information Administration reference case projects an average annual growth rate of electricity demand of between 1.3 and 1.9 percent through 2010. Other forecasts generally fall within that range. U.S. Department of Energy, Energy Information Administration, *Annual Energy Outlook 1993 with Projections to 2010* (Washington, DC: U.S. Government Printing Office, January 1993), pp. 49 and 78.

95. The first test case for license renewal, the Yankee Atomic Electric Company's small (175-megawatt) facility at Rowe, Massachusetts, resulted in Yankee voluntarily closing the plant in 1992.

96. Very little empirical work has been done comparing the full social costs of nuclear and other forms of energy. There are significant problems, for example, in evaluating externalities such as nuclear waste disposal. However, it should be pointed out that the industry believes the waste externality has already been internalized, since utilities pay one-tenth of a cent per kilowatt-hour of nuclear-generated electricity into a fund to develop waste transportation and disposal options.

97. For example, a Gallup poll conducted in July 1990 found that 74 percent of respondents thought the United States should use more nuclear energy if that would cut GHG emissions and air pollution. Polling conducted by Cambridge Reports/Research International in March 1992 found that 60 percent of respondents favored the use of nuclear energy for electricity generation, 73 percent thought nuclear energy had an important role to play in meeting America's future energy needs, and 62 percent favored building new nuclear plants if more electricity was needed in the years ahead.

98. See Task Committee of the Utility Nuclear Power Oversight Committee, *Leadership in Achieving Operational Excellence: The Challenge For All Nuclear Utilities* (August 1986), Appendix A; National Research Council, *Nuclear Power: Technical and Institutional Options for the Future* (Washington, DC: National Academy Press, 1992), p. 62, and Richard E. Balzhiser "Future Consequences of Nuclear Nonpolicy," National Academy of Engineering, *Energy Production, Consumption and Consequences* (Washington, DC: National Academy Press, 1990), p. 195.

99. See U.S. Department of Energy, Energy Information Administration, *An Analysis of Nuclear Plant Operating Costs: A 1991 Update* (Washington, DC: U.S. Government Printing Office, May 1991), pp. 4-6.

100. Science Concepts, Inc., *The Impact of Nuclear Energy on Utility Fuel Use and Utility Atmospheric Emissions 1973-1990* (Chevy Chase, MD: February 1992).

101. A recently released study by the National Research Council concluded that "the risk to the health of the public from the operation of current reactors in the United States is very small." National Research Council, *Nuclear Power: Technical and Institutional Options for the Future*, p. 4.

102. "U.S. to Buy Russian Uranium," *The Washington Post* (September 1, 1992): A1.

103. K. Chung and G. Hazelrigg, "Nuclear Power Technology: A Mandate For Change," *Nuclear Technology* (November 1988).

104. National Research Council, *Nuclear Power: Technical and Institutional Options for the Future*, p. 34.

105. Capital carrying charges are principally the cost of capital plus depreciation and amortization of the costs of construction and finance. They usually also include plant decommissioning costs. National Research Council, *Nuclear Power: Technical and Institutional Options for the Future*, p. 27.

106. National Research Council, *Nuclear Power: Technical and Institutional Options for the Future*, p. 40.

107. The utility would also have to demonstrate that the plant was built to the specifications.

108. The French example is instructive. Instead of having multiple reactor vendors and reactor designs as in the United States, France has a single vendor and architect-engineer and has focused on one technology only: the pressurized water reactor. Construction practices are uniform, and evolutionary design improvements have been incorporated in an orderly process.

109. The industry has selected two of these for funding support of what is referred to as "first-of-a-kind" engineering; that is, detailed engineering plans for that part of the plant outside of the reactor itself. The intent is to standardize not only the reactor but the remainder of the plant as well. The two designs, which will be cofunded by the industry, the manufacturers, and the Department of Energy, are General Electric's 1300 MWe Advanced Boiling Water Reactor (AWBR) and Westinghouse Electric's 600 MWe AP600 Advanced Passive Pressurized Water Reactor.

110. Nuclear Power Oversight Committee, *Position Paper on Standardization* (April 1991), p. 3-1.

111. The Canadian CANDU-3 heavy-water reactor is further along than the passive-safety designs, but it has not yet entered the U.S. design certification process and, according to the National Research Council, it does not offer greater potential than designs already in that process. National Research Council, *Nuclear Power: Technical and Institutional Options for the Future*, pp. 91-155.

112. National Research Council, *Nuclear Power: Technical and Institutional Options for the Future*, p. 151.

113. U.S. Department of Energy, Energy Information Administration, *An Analysis of Nuclear Plant Operating Costs: A 1991 Update*, p. 4. Recent data indicate that the rise in nuclear plant operation and maintenance costs has slowed in the past couple of years. However, the industry concedes that some nuclear power plants will need to show a decline in costs rather than just stabilization in order to remain competitive. See Marvin S. Fertel, "Issues Surrounding the Management of O&M Costs" (Paper presented at American Nuclear Society Executive Conference on Controlling Nuclear Plant Operation and Maintenance Costs: A Matter of Survival, May 1992).

114. Nuclear Regulatory Commission, "Licensed Operating Reactors," NUREG-0020 (Washington, DC: March 1992).

115. Nuclear Power Oversight Committee, *Position Paper on Standardization*, pp. 5-2 and 5-3.

116. For example, in parts of the developing world that lack electricity transmission lines, photovoltaic technology may already be cost-effective, thus providing export opportunities for U.S. manufacturers.

117. Solar Energy Research Institute, *The Potential of Renewable Energy: An Interlaboratory White Paper*, prepared for the U.S. Department of Energy (Golden, CO: Solar Energy Research Institute, March 1990), pp. 31-32.

118. American Wind Energy Association, "Wind Energy — a Resource for the 1990s and Beyond" (AWEA information sheet, February 15, 1991).

119. For fiscal 1992, $242.6 million was appropriated for R&D, compared with $198.4 million in fiscal 1991.

120. "Wind Farms May Energize the Midwest," *The Wall Street Journal* (September 6, 1991): B1.

121. Electric Power Research Institute, "Excellent Forecast for Wind," *EPRI Journal* (June 1990): 23.

122. Solar Energy Research Institute, *The Potential of Renewable Energy: An Interlaboratory White Paper*, p. A-3.

123. Solar Energy Research Institute, *The Potential of Renewable Energy: An Interlaboratory White Paper*, p. C-1.

124. Congress of the United States, Office of Technology Assessment, *Energy Technology Choices: Shaping Our Future* (Washington, DC: U.S. Government Printing Office, July 1991), p. 96.

125. Congress of the United States, Office of Technology Assessment, *Energy Technology Choices: Shaping Our Future*, p. 98.

MEMORANDA OF COMMENT, RESERVATION, OR DISSENT

Page 2, FRANKLIN A. LINDSAY, Retired Chairman, Itek Corporation, with which WILLIAM D. EBERLE, Chairman, Manchester Associates, Ltd., and ELMER B. STAATS, Former Comptroller General of the United States, have asked to be associated.

I strongly support the principal recommendation of this policy statement that market-based mechanisms rather than command-and-control mechanisms be used in government policies to achieve the greatest public benefit for the lowest cost. The report identifies a carbon tax as the most effective way of achieving reductions in greenhouse gas emissions. But it concludes that neither a carbon tax nor any other tax on energy should be imposed until further research establishes beyond reasonable doubt that global warming will have significant damaging effects on life on the planet. This could delay action many years. It would be preferable to put in place a low-cost carbon tax promptly in order to avoid the necessity of more drastic and inefficient controls at a later time.

Unlike other CED statements that have always considered all relevant factors affecting a policy issue, this report, by design, does not. Factors other than the environment will have at least as much relevance to energy tax policy as does the potential for atmospheric warming. A carbon tax or, in varying degrees, other energy taxes applied now will provide added market incentives to improve overall efficiency in the use of fossil fuels, reduce dependence on foreign oil imports, reduce our foreign trade deficit, and add incentives for the more rapid development of renewable and nonpolluting sources, such as photovoltaics, wind energy, or a new generation of inherently safe nuclear reactors.

The report points out that a carbon tax would require many years to significantly affect the role of atmospheric warming, a reason to begin now to cut back emissions. There is enough known now about potential global warming to include it among other objectives as justification for immediate action.

Page 7, LEON C. HOLT, JR., Retired Chairman, Air Products and Chemicals, Inc.

Whether motivated by revenue concerns or environmental advocacy, energy taxes place a disproportionate burden on energy-intensive industries, as well as lead to a preference of one form of energy use over another, which may conflict with sound energy policy. Furthermore, taxes on energy in general are inefficient sources of revenue and tend to raise inflation and interest rates. The corresponding effect on the economy is to affect adversely GNP, employment, business earnings and investment, international competitiveness, and the trade balance.

Page 7, FRANKLIN A. LINDSAY, with which WILLIAM D. EBERLE and ELMER B. STAATS have asked to be associated.

These concerns about the effects of a carbon tax on the competitiveness of U.S. industry certainly do not apply to options such as a gasoline tax. Figure 15 demonstrates that gasoline prices (including taxes) in the United States are a third to a quarter of those in France, Germany, Japan, and the U.K. — our principal export competitors. Surely, an increase in taxes on gasoline has a long way to go before placing the United States at a competitive disadvantage. The recommendations for further study will appear as simply a delaying tactic against reasonable tax increases.

93

Page 8, HAROLD A. POLING, Chairman and Chief Executive Officer, Ford Motor Company, MARTIN B. ZIMMERMAN, Chief Economist, Ford Motor Company, and GEORGE C. EADS, Vice President, Worldwide Economic and Market Analysis, General Motors Corporation, with which ROBERT B. MERCER, Retired Chairman, The Goodyear Tire & Rubber Company, and ROCCO C. SICILIANO, Beverly Hills, California, have asked to be associated.

We agree that, from a purely environmental viewpoint, a gasoline tax is not the most cost-effective measure for dealing either with local pollution or global climate change. However, we believe that, like a carbon fee or an emissions charge, a gasoline tax would have important energy and environmental benefits. Indeed, studies show that in the auto sector, it is about four times more costly to save a gallon of gasoline using command-and-control measures such as CAFE than by increasing the gasoline tax. Therefore, we believe that if additional revenues are needed to supplement spending cuts in order to reduce the budget deficit, a gasoline tax should be among the measures considered.

Page 11 and page 53, RICHARD J. KRUIZENGA, Irving, Texas

It is premature for the U.S. government to develop an elaborate comprehensive contingency plan to reduce greenhouse gas emissions at this time. The science is not sufficiently developed to establish the nature or magnitude of any potential problem, much less to provide the basis for a detailed contingency plan. The priority effort should be on the development of relevant science in a comprehensive and expeditious manner.

Page 19, ROCCO C. SICILIANO

Regarding future energy supplies, the report provides only a limited discussion of natural gas and its potential environmental and economic benefits. It notes in passing the role of past regulatory actions in dampening supply but does not discuss options for addressing these difficulties and reaping the benefits of this fuel source.

Page 35, EDWIN LUPBERGER, Chairman and Chief Executive Officer, Entergy Corporation

The CED recommends internalizing social costs of pollution as an element of production costs and price. I have some concern on this position. As an electric utility, our system has actively pursued the development of an Integrated Resource Plan through discussions with our regulators over the last two years. If "social cost" means a reasonably comprehensive view of marginal cost, then I agree. However, if this recommendation means attempting to "monetize" and internalize externalities as currently being attempted in some states, then I am not willing to endorse this at this time.

Page 41, ROCCO C. SICILIANO

The report suggests that the costs of reducing emissions from mobile sources are higher than the costs associated with cleaning up stationary sources. Given the history of regulation of stationary sources in the Los Angeles area, that assumption is questionable at least for that region. While the report recognizes the need for source equity, it assumes that we are starting from a level playing field rather than acknowledging past levels of pollution abatement and regulatory intervention in each sector. The 1990 Clean Air Act recognized this inequity and attempted to emphasize mobile source controls accordingly.

Page 44, LEON C. HOLT, JR.

This statement appears to take a dim view of scrubber technology. Economics dictate that the least-cost compliance option should be taken regardless of the methodology employed — which may or may not include the use of scrubbers.

Page 64, EDWIN LUPBERGER

I agree with emphasizing DSM programs that do not increase *long-term* unit costs. However, if the recommendation means limiting DSM to programs that pass the ratepayer impact measure (RIM), or "No Losers Test," I do not agree. There needs to be flexibility to go beyond this to accomplish conservation and efficiency goals. All of our retail regulators are requested to adopt the Total Resource Cost (TRC) test as the criterion for judging the cost-effectiveness of DSM programs.

Page 70, ROCCO C. SICILIANO

The report supports federal funding of research and development into promising alternative fuels, but opposes barriers for alternative-fueled vehicles. The use of natural gas in vehicles is a promising technology but must overcome infrastructure mandates that are in part a product of past energy policies. The mandates that have been proposed have been intended to support research and development of this promising technology by developing a critical mass to overcome the "chicken and egg" problems of supply facilities.

OBJECTIVES OF THE COMMITTEE FOR ECONOMIC DEVELOPMENT

For 50 years, the Committee for Economic Development has been a respected influence on the formation of business and public policy. CED is devoted to these two objectives:

To develop, through objective research and informed discussion, findings and recommendations for private and public policy that will contribute to preserving and strengthening our free society, achieving steady economic growth at high employment and reasonably stable prices, increasing productivity and living standards, providing greater and more equal opportunity for every citizen, and improving the quality of life for all.

To bring about increasing understanding by present and future leaders in business, government, and education, and among concerned citizens, of the importance of these objectives and the ways in which they can be achieved.

CED's work is supported by private voluntary contributions from business and industry, foundations, and individuals. It is independent, nonprofit, nonpartisan, and nonpolitical.

Through this business-academic partnership, CED endeavors to develop policy statements and other research materials that commend themselves as guides to public and business policy; that can be used as texts in college economics and political science courses and in management training courses; that will be considered and discussed by newspaper and magazine editors, columnists, and commentators; and that are distributed abroad to promote better understanding of the American economic system.

CED believes that by enabling business leaders to demonstrate constructively their concern for the general welfare, it is helping business to earn and maintain the national and community respect essential to the successful functioning of the free enterprise capitalist system.

STATEMENTS ON NATIONAL POLICY ISSUED BY THE COMMITTEE FOR ECONOMIC DEVELOPMENT

SELECTED PUBLICATIONS:

Why Child Care Matters: Preparing Young Children for a More Productive America *(1993)*

Restoring Prosperity: Budget Choices for Economic Growth *(1992)*

The United States in the New Global Economy: A Rallier of Nations *(1992)*

The Economy and National Defense: Adjusting to Cutbacks in the Post-Cold War Era *(1991)*

Politics, Tax Cuts and the Peace Dividend *(1991)*

The Unfinished Agenda: A New Vision for Child Development and Education *(1991)*

Foreign Investment in the United States: What Does It Signal? *(1990)*

An America That Works: The Life-Cycle Approach to a Competitive Work Force *(1990)*

Breaking New Ground in U.S. Trade Policy *(1990)*

Battling America's Budget Deficits *(1989)*

*Strengthening U.S.-Japan Economic Relations *(1989)*

Who Should Be Liable? A Guide to Policy for Dealing with Risk *(1989)*

Investing in America's Future: Challenges and Opportunities for Public Sector Economic Policies *(1988)*

Children in Need: Investment Strategies for the Educationally Disadvantaged *(1987)*

Finance and Third World Economic Growth *(1987)*

Toll of the Twin Deficits *(1987)*

Reforming Health Care: A Market Prescription *(1987)*

Work and Change: Labor Market Adjustment Policies in a Competitive World *(1987)*

Leadership for Dynamic State Economies *(1986)*

Investing in our Children: Business and the Public Schools *(1985)*

Fighting Federal Deficits: The Time for Hard Choices *(1985)*

Strategy for U.S. Industrial Competitiveness *(1984)*

Strengthening the Federal Budget Process: A Requirement for Effective Fiscal Control *(1983)*

Productivity Policy: Key to the Nation's Economic Future *(1983)*

Energy Prices and Public Policy *(1982)*

Public-Private Partnership: An Opportunity for Urban Communities *(1982)*

Reforming Retirement Policies *(1981)*

Transnational Corporations and Developing Countries: New Policies for a Changing World Economy *(1981)*

Fighting Inflation and Rebuilding a Sound Economy *(1980)*

Stimulating Technological Progress (1980)

Helping Insure Our Energy Future: A Program for Developing Synthetic Fuel Redefining Government's Role in the Market System (1979)

Improving Management of the Public Work Force: The Challenge to State and Local Government (1978)

Jobs for the Hard-to-Employ: New Directions for a Public-Private Partnership *(1978)*

An Approach to Federal Urban Policy *(1977)*

Key Elements of a National Energy Strategy *(1977)*

Nuclear Energy and National Security *(1976)*

Fighting Inflation and Promoting Growth *(1976)*

Improving Productivity in State and Local Government *(1976)*

*International Economic Consequences of High-Priced Energy *(1975)*

Achieving Energy Independence *(1974)*

---

*Statements issued in association with CED counterpart organizations in foreign countries.

CED COUNTERPART ORGANIZATIONS

Close relations exist between the Committee for Economic Development and independent, nonpolitical research organizations in other countries. Such counterpart groups are composed of business executives and scholars and have objectives similar to those of CED, which they pursue by similarly objective methods. CED cooperates with these organizations on research and study projects of common interest to the various countries concerned. This program has resulted in a number of joint policy statements involving such international matters as energy, East-West trade, assistance to developing countries, and the reduction of nontariff barriers to trade.

CE	Circulo de Empresarios Madrid, Spain
CEDA	Committee for Economic Development of Australia Sydney, Australia
CEPES	Vereinigung für Wirtschaftlichen Fortschritt E.V. Frankfurt, Germany
FORUM	Forum de Administradores de Empresas Lisbon, Portugal
IE	Institut de L'Entreprise Brussels, Belgium
IE	Institut de l'Entreprise Paris, France
IEA	Institute of Economic Affairs London, England
IW	Institut der Deutschen Wirtschaft Cologne, Germany
経済同友会	Keizai Doyukai Tokyo, Japan
SNS	Studieförbundet Naringsliv och Samhälle Stockholm, Sweden